Everything

your baby would ask…

*…if only he or
she could talk*

KYRA KARMILOFF AND
ANNETTE KARMILOFF-SMITH

Everything
your baby would ask…

*…if only he or
she could talk*

WARD LOCK

A WARD LOCK BOOK
This edition first published in the United Kingdom by
Ward Lock
Wellington House
125 Strand
London WC2R 0BB

A Cassell imprint

First published 1998

CREATED AND PRODUCED BY
CARROLL & BROWN LIMITED
20 LONSDALE ROAD
LONDON NW6 6RD

PUBLISHING DIRECTOR DENIS KENNEDY
ART DIRECTOR CHRISSIE LLOYD

MANAGING EDITOR RACHEL ARIS
SENIOR ART EDITORS MANISHA PATEL, ADELLE MORRIS
DESIGNER RACHEL GOLDSMITH

PHOTOGRAPHERS JULES SELMES, MIKE GOOD

PRODUCTION WENDY ROGERS, KAREN KLOOT
COMPUTER MANAGEMENT JOHN CLIFFORD, PAUL STRADLING

British Library Catalogue-in-Publication Data
A catalogue record for this book is available from the British Library

ISBN 0–7063–7573–4

REPRODUCED BY COLOURSCAN, SINGAPORE
PRINTED IN ITALY BY CHROMOLITHO

Contents

✴ ✴

Preface

* *

Have you ever wondered what is going on in babies' minds before they can talk? What do they understand about the social and physical worlds? Is it all a complete mystery, or are babies born with some knowledge of what to expect? Is their life in utero totally passive, merely swimming around in the amniotic liquid until it is time to come out, or are they already learning something during their intrauterine stay? When do babies recognise their parents' faces and voices? How important is play in learning about the conventions of social life? How does the baby experiment with language and objects? These and many other questions are addressed in this book.

* *

Don't think that this is your typical 'How to bring up your baby' book, however. You won't find advice on nappy changing or when to introduce solid food. Our aim is different and, we believe, much more crucial for understanding how your baby develops. We try to penetrate the baby's mind and guess at the questions babies might ask about themselves and their experiences if only they could talk — to see the world from the baby's perspective. For if you are to be a confident parent, grandparent or child-carer, you need to understand how each baby gradually becomes an intelligent, independent individual.

* *

Each chapter of the book focuses on a broad area of infant development. The amusing question—answer format (baby asks a question, we provide an answer) is followed by slightly more serious text, telling you about the kind of research that has helped us discover how babies develop. We have mostly concentrated on life in utero and in infancy, but at times we have added a 'Looking Ahead' section where we felt it was important to explore how the behaviour of babies gradually evolves through toddlerhood and beyond. We have also included dozens of suggestions for ways you can make your own amazing discoveries about your baby's development, as well as special features on the increasingly specialised workings of the infant brain. Imagine, your baby's brain is more active and consumes more energy than yours! And science now has techniques for looking at infants' brain activity.

* *

There can be huge differences between one infant's rate of development and another's, and the ages we give in this book are simply rough guides. Your baby will find his or her own schedule of development and you should only be worried if milestones occur well outside the age ranges we provide. Using 'he or she' always sounds heavy, so we decided not to keep doing this in the rest of the book. But each mum and dad obviously cares about whether they have a boy or a girl and they certainly don't want their baby referred to as 'it'! We opted for a compromise whereby we refer to the baby as male in one chapter and female in the next.

* *

Finally, a little about the voices behind this book. Your two authors were actually three: Kyra was expecting her first baby while writing this book, so we had a constant eavesdropper! And many years ago, Kyra was Annette's second baby. We have worked together before, but this is our first project as a fully fledged daughter–mother team. We both enjoyed the experience immensely and plan further joint books. At the end of writing not only have we not fallen out under the strain, but we've actually become even closer friends.

* *

The book is dedicated to Annette's four tiny grand-children: to Misha, the baby son of Gideon and Kyra, born six days after we handed in the final manuscript; to Alexander and Nicholas, the baby sons of Enrico and Yara, Annette's elder daughter; and to Théïa, the baby daughter of Paul and Cléa, Annette's step-daughter. We hope that you will enjoy reading the book as much as we've enjoyed writing it.

Kyra Karmiloff and Annette Karmiloff-Smith

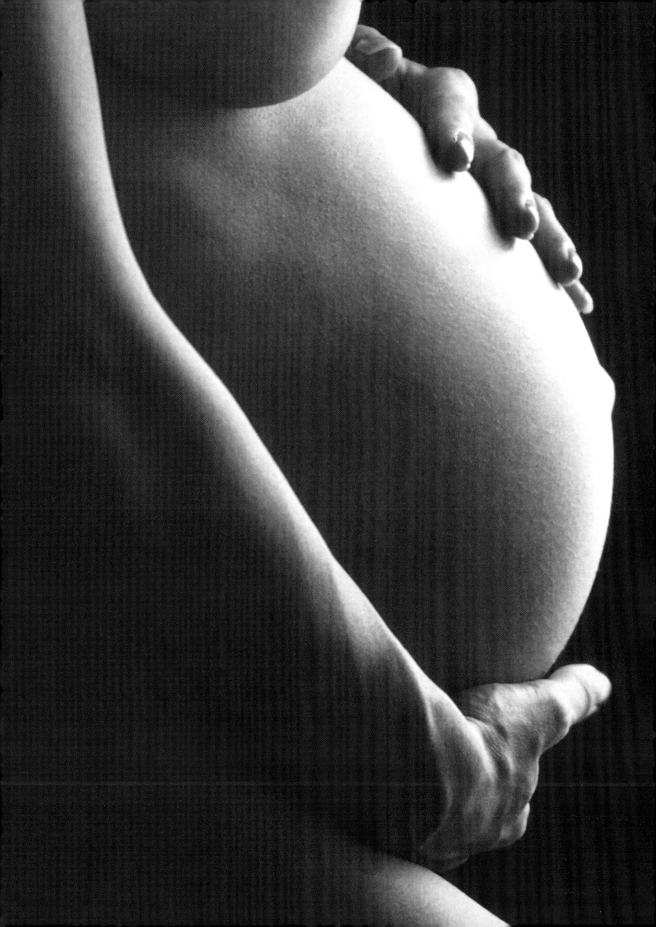

My Life in Utero

Until recently, life in the womb remained a total mystery. We knew nothing about what unborn babies could perceive, how they reacted to different kinds of sounds or emotions, nor which sex they would be. Nowadays, with ultrasound scans and exciting new experimental techniques, researchers have discovered a great deal about how the foetus develops and what she experiences in the womb. If they wish, parents can now find out the sex of their infant well before birth, as well as whether they are expecting one or several children. On the monitor, they can see and hear their infant's heart beating quite clearly and can watch the baby tossing and turning in utero. If there are twins, parents can watch the interaction between the two babies. Researchers have discovered many things about how the unborn baby spends her time floating in the amniotic liquid, how she is fed, how she acquires some knowledge of the outside world and how the mother's actions can affect her development.

Most of the limbs and the major organs of the baby's body — such as the heart, the lungs, the kidneys and the bladder — are formed during the first three months or trimester of pregnancy and then gradually grow in size. Although around the sixth week of gestational age the heart is still far from being fully formed, amazingly it nonetheless starts to beat around this time. And by the eighth week, the eyes, nostrils and mouth start to take form. At the same time, the foetal brain undergoes rapid change. Although the complex

network of connections between brain cells only develops significantly after birth, the formation of the individual cells and their
migration to different regions of the brain takes place during
prenatal life. Incredible as it may seem, the foetus produces 250
new brain cells every minute! The process of cell formation is
complete by the seventh month of gestation and at that point
the baby possesses almost the full complement of brain cells that
she will have throughout the rest of her life. Only a few parts
of the brain, such as the olfactory bulbs that govern our sense of
smell, continue to add cells during postnatal life. So while life in
utero is crucial for the growth and migration of brain cells, the
period after birth is the time for the major building of connections
between these cells. These connections are important because on their
own the cells are limited in what they can do. When connected to one
another, however, they can send messages across the brain, bringing
different regions to work in concert, and produce intelligent behaviour.

· ·

One of the most exciting advances to take place in child development research
has been the recent discovery that babies actually begin
learning about the world while they're still in utero.
Hearing is the easiest of the senses for scientists to
assess, so most of what we know about foetuses'
capacity to learn concerns the final trimester of
intrauterine life because by this time the auditory
system is well developed. Researchers have now
pinpointed the extraordinary sensitivities the
foetus has to her mother's heartbeat, to music
and particularly to her mother's voice. It is
also during the last trimester that the foetus
shows a whole range of motor behaviour
(physical activities) and starts to regulate
her pattern of waking and sleeping cycles.

Life in the womb is far from passive. In between periods of sleep, the foetus actively sucks her thumb, holds on to the umbilical cord, frequently changes position and reacts to all kinds of sounds, tastes, strong light changes and pressure on the mother's abdomen, as well as emotions that pass from mother to child. It's hard to believe that in the last three months of pregnancy the tiny creature growing inside you is already eavesdropping on your conversations, listening to changes in language and to the differences between male and female voices, and witnessing your mood changes. Of course, she does not actually understand what you are saying, hearing or feeling, but she does associate changes in the tone of your voice with other physiological clues about what you are experiencing.

The final months of pregnancy are a time when you can start to develop a sort of dialogue with your unborn baby and thereby begin the wonderful process of bonding. You will find if you carefully monitor your baby's movements that you can tell whether she is stimulated or soothed by the music you are listening to or by the conversations you are having. She may also react to a change in your diet, and sense whether you are in a great hurry or feeling contented and relaxed. Take time to tune into your baby's movements, and you will be getting to know each other well before the magic moment when you meet for the first time in the outside world.

Where does my food come from?

*I seem to be growing and getting stronger
every day, and I just love doing acrobatics.
But I'm not eating anything at all, so where
does all my energy come from, and how come
my body doesn't need food?*

*During your life in the womb, your physical well-being
is exclusively catered for by your mum's own body.
With the help of the placenta and the umbilical cord,
everything your developing body and brain require to
grow and function is passed from her bloodstream into
yours. So don't worry about food just yet, you are
safely 'plugged in' to a constant supply of nutrients
and energy stores that will stop you getting peckish
and keep you healthy and active.*

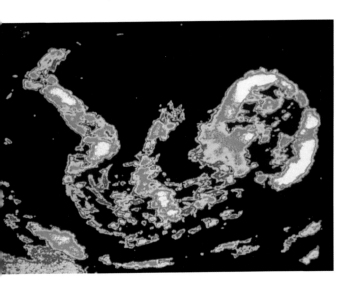

*During the baby's life in the
amniotic sac, she spends much
time manoeuvring around her
watery home. Her athletic
activities are fuelled by
nutrients supplied by her
mother via the umbilical cord.*

KEEPING BABY ALIVE The womb is a unique and
complex environment that nurtures and protects the
baby within. The changing needs of the developing
foetus are carefully monitored by her mother's body
through minute changes in the balance between the
make-up of her blood and that of her baby. Even a tiny
increase in the levels of one constituent of the baby's
blood – a hormone, a chemical, or a waste product,
for example – triggers a response in the mother's
body. This intricate feedback mechanism ensures that
the baby has access to all the oxygen, nutrients, vitamins and minerals she needs to grow and develop.

The organ sustaining the baby is the placenta – a
very complex structure which, by the time the baby
is born, can be as large as a soup bowl and weigh up
to 0.45 kg (over 1 lb). Shaped like a basin, it is a meeting point for maternal and foetal blood and, as such,
acts as the baby's source of nourishment during life in
utero. Inside the placenta, the two bloodstreams flow
next to each other, separated only by the thinnest
layer of cells. Through these cells, a special exchange
is carried out. Simultaneously, oxygen and nourishment from the mother's body are released into the
baby's bloodstream, while waste products from the
baby's body (such as carbon monoxide) are released
into her bloodstream and carried away for disposal.
Blood itself never passes between mother and baby.

The placenta also acts as a vital protective
barrier against any infections and poisons present in
the mother's blood system, although unfortunately
such protection isn't total. It is here, too, that the
hormones oestrogen and progesterone are regulated. These have a specific
role in preparing the mother's body for the onset and maintenance of pregnancy, as well as playing a part in triggering the mechanism of childbirth.

The baby is linked to the placenta via an intricate bundle of vessels that
constitute the umbilical cord. While this cord happens to provide the foetus
with one of her only 'toys' inside the womb (*see page 22*), it in fact represents
no less than the baby's lifeline. Consisting of two arteries and a vein coiled

around each other and covered by a firm, protective, jelly-like membrane, it is remarkably strong and can sustain any amount of squeezing and twisting by the baby. The force of the blood rushing through the vessels keeps it extended enough to prevent kinking or knotting, so it is relatively difficult for it to get tangled around the baby's neck. As the uterus expands over the course of the pregnancy, the cord grows rapidly in both length and width so that the foetus can move as freely as possible within the womb. By full term, the cord is usually at least as long as the baby herself, who will soon no longer need it. Once she is born and can breathe for herself, the cord is cut by a doctor; from then on, her organs have to fend for themselves.

SAFEGUARDING BABY'S HEALTH From the minute their pregnancies are confirmed, mothers-to-be are given extensive dietary advice by doctors and midwives concerning what and how much to eat, and what to avoid. A great deal is now known about the benefits or adverse effects of certain foods, vitamins and minerals and, while it may seem daunting at first, such advice should always be taken very seriously. This is not to say that a pregnant woman should completely transform her diet, but she should ensure that she eats at least some of the necessary nutrients and vitamins each day. The placenta can only nourish the baby with what is present in the maternal bloodstream. At the same time, the mother's body protects itself by conserving some level of essential nutrients. So if she suffers from deficiencies, it is likely that her baby will too. We have all heard the saying 'You are what you eat' – well, when referring to a developing baby it would be more appropriate to say, 'You are what your mother eats!'

Research has shown that there are no completely safe levels of smoking, drinking, or drug-taking for pregnant women, as these can have far-reaching effects on the foetus in terms of lowered birth-weight, slower physical development and even reduced IQ. In fact, what the foetus receives through her mother's blood can affect not only her growth rate in general, but also the *way* her brain and body develop, which can't always be altered by subsequent improvements in nutrition. Scientists have proposed that the human body, from its very beginnings inside the womb, may form a 'memory' of early nutritional experiences and that this may have an impact on its subsequent development and temperament. It is still unknown precisely how this takes place.

Why does mum always say 'no' when people offer her a drink or a cigarette. Has she always been so health-conscious?

Now that she has you to worry about, your mum's being very careful about what she puts into her body. The nicotine from cigarettes reduces the amount of oxygen that reaches you through her blood. Alcohol is also harmful: it can damage your growing organs, which is why she's not going to get tipsy over the next few months.

What's that horrible thing I can taste? Oh no – don't tell me mum's been eating too much garlic again?

The amniotic fluid in which you are floating can sometimes take on the taste of a particular food or drink that your mum has consumed. Over the next few months, you'll find yourself becoming accustomed to certain tastes, and liking these more than others. Such preferences will continue once you're born: you might even recognise some of your favourite tastes in your mum's breast milk.

ACQUIRING A SENSE OF TASTE During pregnancy, a baby will regularly fill her mouth with the amniotic liquid in which she floats – not for food, of course, but simply while she swims around. By the time she reaches six months' gestation, taste buds will have developed in her mouth and she will be able to tell whether the liquid tastes bitter, sweet or sour. This marks the beginning of her taste preferences.

The amniotic fluid in which the baby floats is renewed constantly, about once every three hours, via the placenta. Consisting mostly of water (98–99 per cent), it also contains some hormones, proteins and other nutrients. Astonishingly, substances can cross the placenta to season the fluid with the taste of the mother's last meal! Research has indicated that unborn babies show a preference for sweet-tasting fluid and, if their mothers rarely have spicy food, will find spices unpalatable. So if mum has been out for an unusually garlicky meal, a baby may show her objection by grimacing once the fluid takes on the taste of mum's dinner.

It is thought that by becoming familiar with those tastes most often present in their intrauterine environments, babies prepare themselves for the special flavour of their mothers' milk. Indeed, mothers who change their diets dramatically once their babies are born can have difficulty getting their infants to accept their breast milk, as its taste will be unfamiliar and uninviting. Rather amazingly, as the baby experiences different flavours, she makes clever associations between the taste and the effects the substance has on her mother. If her mother drinks a strong cup of coffee, for example, the baby's breathing and heart rate may increase to mirror her mother's own response to the caffeine. Even more cleverly, she will react in exactly the same way if mum later drinks a cup of decaffeinated coffee, because she has learned to associate the general taste of coffee with a specific physical response. Unborn babies are clearly more switched on than we once thought!

What are all these sounds I can hear?

It's lovely and snug in here, but it does get quite noisy at times. I can hear strange gurgles and swishing noises, a beat coming from somewhere above me and all sorts of other things that come and go. What are all these weird sounds echoing around me?

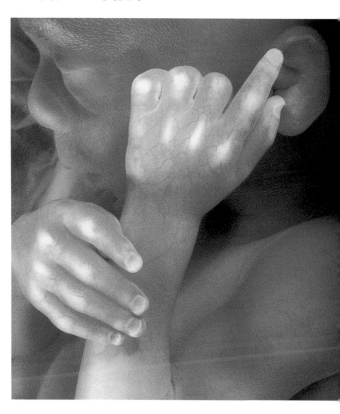

The multitude of 'weird sounds' that reach your ears are the noises your mum's body is making as it goes about its non-stop business. Though you're not aware of it, even the organs in your own little body are making similar noises. The sounds you hear in the womb are a very special experience that you'll never have again once you're born.

SENSITIVITY TO NOISE A baby's sense of hearing develops as early as 15–20 weeks' gestation. Inside the womb, the baby is surrounded by a rich orchestra of sounds produced by the continuous activity of her mother's organs, as well as noises from the outside world. By 25 weeks, a sound emitted from a loud-speaker placed on the stomach of a pregnant woman produces a jerky movement from her foetus. New experiences in utero, such as hearing a strange sound, also cause the baby's heart to beat faster. Although we know the foetus is able to hear sounds as early as 15 weeks, it is only at 25 weeks that ultrasound images can show that she is actually reacting to what she hears with an immediate startle response, and not just moving arbitrarily.

In the last three months of intrauterine life, babies' brains are busy processing a whole world of sounds. Scientists have been able to record what the baby can hear by placing a tiny microphone close to the uterus, and the results are quite amazing. We often imagine a baby curled up asleep in the warm, silent environment of her mother's womb. But in reality, her little world is filled with a whole range of different sounds that echo through the amniotic liquid. The swishing of her mother's blood going past the placenta, for example, is a little like the sound we hear when we put a seashell up to our ear. But the baby also hears her mother's heart beating, the gasses bubbling and moving around her digestive system, her breathing as air fills the lungs above the womb – not to mention the occasional sneeze, hiccup or burp!

HOW DO WE KNOW? WINDOWS ON THE SECRET WORLD OF THE UNBORN BABY

Scientists used to think it was impossible to test the capabilities of children before they were able to speak. But researchers have recently developed several ingenious ways to ask questions of the foetus and prelinguistic newborn. Since the advent of ultrasound, we have been able to study the development of movement and sleep patterns in the foetus. Through this scanning technique, patterns of sound waves are translated by computer into visual images. This has allowed researchers to examine what foetuses are doing and how they are developing from very early on in gestation. Using scans to record kicking or startle reflexes and heart monitors to measure changes in heart rate, researchers can now assess foetal reactions and capabilities. For example, if a loudspeaker playing a recurring sound is placed on a pregnant woman's abdomen during the last trimester of her pregnancy and the sound is suddenly changed, her baby's heart rate or kicking rate will change too, indicating that the baby is already actively processing sound differences through her sense of hearing. Similarly, if a bright light is shone onto the surface of the pregnant belly, the foetus will react by increasing her movements – revealing that the baby's visual system has started to develop.

More complex techniques have been devised to assess newborn faculties; these measure two things in particular – what the newborn remembers from her life in utero and what she can do before she starts learning from life outside the womb. One technique makes use of the sucking reflex to identify a newborn's preferences. The infant is given a non-nutritive dummy which is attached to

a computer that measures the baby's sucking rate. A certain sucking rate causes the computer to play her mother's voice, but when the baby lowers her sucking rate, a strange woman's voice is heard instead. In order to bring back her mother's voice, which she prefers, she learns to suck harder again. The computer registers the preferential sucking rate. This tells scientists that the baby learned to recognise her mother's voice while still in utero. Other research has shown that newborns can discriminate at birth between male and female voices, and between the voices of children and adults.

Another technique uses increases in 'looking time'. For instance, a newborn might be shown two displays, at a distance close enough for her to focus on – one of a face-like stimulus (two blobs like eyes and one blob for the nose/mouth area) and the other of the same pattern upside down. She will show her attraction to faces by looking longer at the face-like stimulus. Researchers use these differences in looking time and sucking rate to determine what the newborn might be sensitive to at birth and what a baby is capable of learning inside the womb.

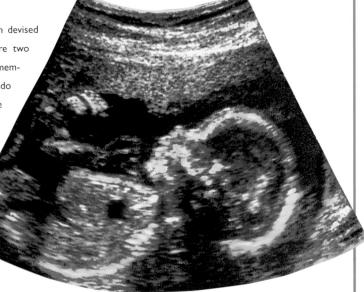

Modern scanning techniques can reveal a great deal about a baby's progress and development in utero, even when the baby is as young as 20 weeks.

Life inside the womb is very stimulating for a baby, and plays an important role in the complex development of her brain and the senses. As she processes the sounds she hears, her brain and body – which are both growing at an incredible rate – become increasingly attuned to one another. This allows certain skills to develop, skills that are vital for human survival but which we take for granted. For example, as the sense of hearing becomes increasingly refined, a baby begins to learn to locate the source of a sound. We have all seen how newborns turn their heads, albeit clumsily, in the direction of a sound. What is amazing is that premature babies who are born between 32 and 35 weeks' gestation and share the same abilities as a foetus of that age still in the womb, already display this skill. The ability to locate where a sound is coming from is crucial for communication, as well as for general survival. So, intrauterine life, although unique and very different from the world we know, prepares the human baby for life outside the womb by providing a range of experiences that are vital for her development.

RECOGNISING THE MATERNAL VOICE Of the many things an unborn baby experiences in utero, perhaps the most stimulating to her is the sound of her mother's voice which, though muffled, can be clearly heard through the amniotic fluid. The growing foetus has an early taste of the world of words. In the last three months of gestation, she spends much of her waking life tuning into the unique melody of her mother speaking. Babies are born with an invaluable little store of knowledge. Imagine how wonderful it would be if they could tell us their secret memories of life in the womb!

Prenatal experiences play an important role in helping the newborn make the transition to the outside world. By the time a baby is born, for example, she is able to use her experiences in the womb to distinguish between her mother's voice and that of anyone else. These other voices sound strange, and take some getting used to. In response to a voice she doesn't know, the newborn's heartbeat may quicken, or she may become more active by moving her legs and arms. In contrast, her mother's voice is soothing to her, something she has heard many times before. So, only moments after birth she can demonstrate an already well-established preference for her mother's voice, even though it now

There's one special sound I hear quite often. It has interesting patterns and rhythms and, I'm not sure why, but I like it more than any of the other noises I hear. Hello, is there somebody else in here with me?

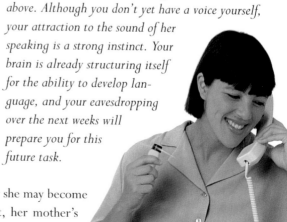

Alas, what you're hearing isn't the voice of a playmate nearby. The special sound is your mum's voice reaching you across the wall of the womb from her voice box above. Although you don't yet have a voice yourself, your attraction to the sound of her speaking is a strong instinct. Your brain is already structuring itself for the ability to develop language, and your eavesdropping over the next weeks will prepare you for this future task.

sounds very different. This is quite amazing because it implies that the foetus not only registers how her mother's voice sounds as a whole, but can also discern the individual qualities, tones and rhythms that are unique to the maternal voice. It is these special characteristics that make it possible for newborns immediately to recognise their mum's voice outside the amniotic liquid of the womb.

Language presents a special challenge to the developing brain because it is a highly complex system vital to human communication and socialisation. The complexity of human language – whether written or spoken – is one of the things that makes us so different from other species, and we begin to prepare for language even before we are born. From inside the womb, the foetus listens in to her mother's conversations, gradually getting used to the special sound of her voice, as well as registering the many different patterns of sounds that make up words and sentences. By becoming familiar early on with the special qualities of language, the baby is born with the ability to distinguish language from other sounds. Of course she cannot actually understand what she is hearing, but experiencing the sound of speech is another important step in foetal development. While a baby's introduction to language inside the womb is vital preparation for the development of language later on, becoming familiar with her mother's unique voice before birth also plays an important role in the bonding process, which begins only seconds after birth when mother and baby meet for the first time. The natural response of parents is to speak lovingly to their tiny newborn.

The other day, while I was happily listening in on mum's conversation, I heard something unfamiliar. The sounds were put together in a strange way and there were patterns and rhythms I didn't recognise. Yet it was still her voice. Is there something you haven't told me about this speaking business?

What you heard were the conversations your mum was having with someone else. These exchanges can be very different in length, style and even language, and you will become increasingly sensitive to these subtle changes. But be patient, the 'speaking business' is one of the most complex things you will learn about as you grow up in the world, and what you experience now, in the womb, is just the beginning!

OTHER VOICES AND LANGUAGES An unborn baby not only listens to her mother's voice but can also hear the sound of other voices nearby – much as when we detect the sound of a conversation going on in another room but cannot hear exactly what is being said. Compared to her mother's voice, the other voices that penetrate the amniotic fluid are more like background noise. However, these conversations provide the baby with a wealth of different and exciting experiences; she may also get to hear what other languages sound like.

If an expectant mother speaks English in her day-to-day life and an Italian friend drops in for a chat, her baby is in for something completely new: 'Ciao, Carla, come stai?' Towards the end of the pregnancy, the sound of a foreign language can instigate an immediate reaction in the foetus. Her heartbeat may quicken, or she may begin to kick more vigorously as she responds to the new experience. It is not just the strangeness of the new words that causes her to become more alert. Rather it is the new sound patterns, intonations and stresses of the foreign language that are unfamiliar.

Over the months, the growing foetus becomes increasingly used to the special qualities of her mother's first language, which she hears most often in the womb. But although it is believed that babies do show a preference at birth for their 'mother tongue', they are actually born equipped with the ability to distinguish *every one* of the 150 individual speech sounds that make up the entire range of human languages.

Research has indicated that newborn babies show a preference for listening to what is already familiar to them. By reading to her toddler his favourite book each day, a pregnant woman may find that, once born, her new baby will also pay particular attention to this story.

You may have noticed that younger children find it much easier to pick up languages than adults. For example, whereas a Japanese adult may find it very hard to distinguish between the words 'lace' and 'race' (there are no separate sounds for 'l' and 'r' in Japanese), a Japanese baby will have no difficulty in picking up the subtle distinctions between different sounds in English, French, Arabic or any other language. It is only after months of repeated exposure to one particular language that babies seem to lose the ability to make distinctions that are not part of their own language. They then become more selective little linguists; this is discussed in more detail on pages 94 and 100–3.

RESPONDING TO MUSIC The filtered sound of music is fascinating to an unborn baby, and it can play a significant role in foetal development. We aren't always aware of just how much of our lives are accompanied by musical sounds: there is music in the background of almost every television programme, and it is often the first thing that greets us when we enter a shop. It's also easy to forget that during the last few weeks of pregnancy, the little one inside you is sharing many of your experiences. So, in fact, when you put your feet up for a little musical break, your foetus may also be relaxing to the same sounds.

Foetal responses to music are not automatic or reflex actions. Rather, music leads to different types of emotional responses in the baby: it can cause stimulation and excitement, or have a sedating, relaxing effect. From as early as 32 weeks' gestation, an unborn baby can form a memory of an item of

I love this tune: it's so relaxing. What makes this particular piece of music so pleasant?

Don't set your music tastes too soon: the preference you currently seem to show for Bach over the Beatles is thanks largely to the fact that you can hear classical music more clearly than pop over the myriad other sounds that echo through the womb. What's more, certain types of music, such as piano and choral music, have sound patterns of a frequency similar to your mum's voice, so you'll probably like these best of all.

music she hears every day, and will recognise it even after birth. Many mothers have reported that their favourite song or piece of music seemed to have an immediate calming effect on their newborn babies.

Amazingly, if the movement patterns of your foetus were monitored while she was listening to the music with which she has become familiar, you would see that after some time her movements would start 'keeping the beat'. As she coordinates her reactions with what she is hearing, the foetus settles into a pattern of regular swimming movements in time with the music. But this is more than just rhythm-keeping. Rather than practising groovy moves for future disco outings, your baby is actually displaying a sophisticated form of logic building – creating complicated links between what she hears and what she does, learning about sound patterns, remembering what she is experiencing and using those memories to respond to future experiences.

The foetus soon becomes quite selective in the music she chooses to react to. Although at 32 weeks' gestation the unborn baby may generally react to musical sounds, it isn't until 38 weeks that she begins to distinguish between different styles of music. This isn't exactly an early indication of musical taste, but familiarity with particular pieces of music can lead to foetuses displaying a form of preference. Your baby will probably get very confused, for example, if you play your favourite Elvis song and change it halfway through to Mozart. The change will make no sense to her, and the confusion may either make her agitated, or alternatively become very still as she works out how to react appropriately to the new sound.

So, next time you get a bit carried away impersonating your favourite pop star, singing along to your favourite song, remember...you're not alone: there's a little person inside you eavesdropping on the whole performance!

Sharing the experience

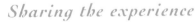

The last few months of pregnancy can be quite exhausting for you as your growing baby places ever-increasing demands on your body. It can be extremely beneficial to you both if you take half an hour regularly each day to put your feet up and listen to music. Choose a piece of music or a song that you find particularly enjoyable and relaxing, and play it during this resting period. Your baby will be tuning in as well.

Once your baby is born, try playing the same piece of music or song in order to calm her down if she is distressed or seems to be having some trouble getting to sleep. Many parents have reported amazing results from this simple and enjoyable experiment.

Is there anything to play with in here?

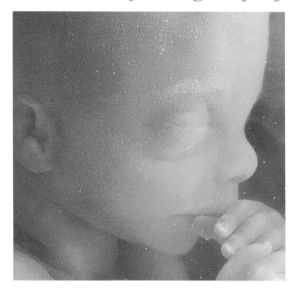

I often go to sleep with my thumb in my mouth and find it still there when I wake up. I don't feel the slightest bit hungry, and it doesn't taste particularly good – so why do I have this urge to keep sucking my thumb?

What you are doing is a normal and very important part of your development. As your different senses awaken, everything around you becomes an active part of your journey of discovery. The urge you have to put something in your mouth and suck hard on it is called the 'sucking reflex', which you'll need to survive in the outside world when you do start feeling hungry. So, when you first come across your mother's breast or the teat of a bottle, you'll already be an expert sucker.

THE SUCKING REFLEX This very strong instinct is one of the most important survival skills with which your baby is born, and is evident from the first seconds after birth. It is amazing how quickly babies learn exactly what to do when they first come into contact with a nipple: they seem so well practised at the business of feeding. This is because the sucking reflex emerges during foetal development. In the womb, all the nutrients necessary for the baby's survival and growth are supplied directly through the umbilical cord from the mother's body into the bloodstream of the foetus, so there is no actual need for feeding skills. But this is still a good time for a foetus to explore and practise some of the skills so vital for life in the outside world, which is why your unborn baby may spend much of her resting time sucking her thumb.

In sucking her thumb, your baby not only prepares for her first feast, but also discovers interesting things about her own body: the feel of her skin and the size of her thumb. You'll see on pages 167–8 how, at a certain age, babies begin putting everything they pick up into their mouths. Again, this is not an indication that supper is long overdue! Rather, their ever-growing curiosity leads babies to want to find out how everything feels and tastes. The tongue is a very sensitive organ with a huge number of nerve endings which, at this stage, register textures in much more detail than infants' clumsy fingers. When babies put objects into their mouths, they also learn about differences in size and shape. So, by sucking her thumb inside your womb, your baby is taking her first steps towards using her sense of touch to explore the world.

Babies continue to suck their fingers or thumbs long after they leave the womb. Not only is the mouth an important means of exploring (see pages 167–8), but sucking itself provides happy memories of being breast-fed, making it a great self-comforter.

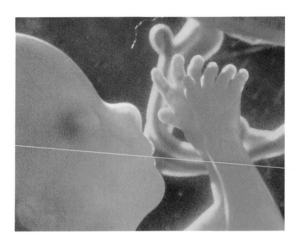

The other day I found this long cord attached to my belly. Although it seems to be part of me, I can't make it move like my arms and legs. And when I grab hold of it, nothing much happens. Can you tell me more about this snaky thing?

What you can feel is the umbilical cord, which supplies your growing body with nourishment and takes away the waste products. In addition to the tactile pleasures it offers, you can probably hear the whoosh of blood as it pulsates through the cord.

EXPLORING THROUGH TOUCH Though the womb is rich with sound, there is relatively little to squeeze, touch and pull on. The texture and shape of the umbilical cord offers the baby quite a different experience from the feel of a thumb in her mouth. The cord is long, with a grooved surface, and can bend in all sorts of ways. In contrast, the thumb is small, quite rigid and the foetus controls its movements. It may not seem such an entertaining game to us, but discovering such things plays an important role in the development of the senses and the brain. By playing in this way, with anything available, the foetus makes the most of what the uterine environment can offer.

Sometimes when I move my legs, I hit something that kicks me back, or it moves and I'm forced to change positions because I'm being squashed. Have I got a roommate?

Yes you have. She's your twin, and you will share mum's womb until it's time for the two of you to be born. As you both came from the same egg, you have the same genetic make-up. This means you look alike and, at the moment, even have identical brains. Once you're born, however, each of you will have your own experiences that will result in differences in the connections that develop in your brains.

TWINS Multiple births are relatively rare, although modern infertility treatments have contributed to an increase in the number of twins, triplets, quadruplets, quintuplets and even septuplets. There are two types of twins: identical twins, which result from the splitting of a single egg at conception, and fraternal twins, which come from the fertilisation of two eggs. Fraternal twins can be of the same or opposite sex and are no more similar in genes than other brothers and sisters from the same parents. Identical twins present quite a different story. As they result from a single egg, their genetic make-up is exactly the same. They are always the same sex, look almost identical, and share many other qualities throughout life.

Recent advances in the effective use of scans have started to reveal fascinating facts about shared intrauterine experiences. From the first stirrings of life, twins move around in the same liquid world, hear the same sounds, compete for space, and therefore impact on each other's movements. They are also affected in similar ways by other modifications in the intrauterine environment, such as changes in mother's diet, in her moods and in her resting and waking patterns. It is not surprising, then, that at birth both identical and fraternal twin babies show similar preferences and behavioural patterns. Up to now, both their brains have been stimulated by the same things and have developed in similar ways. But from the very moment of delivery, their experiences begin to diverge as each embarks on his or her individual life. The birth itself, for instance, will be quite a different experience for each baby: the first born will at times facilitate the subsequent delivery. The atmosphere in the delivery room will also differ, however subtly, as each baby is born. So, from their first breaths, even the most minute differences in their experiences of the outside world will affect the way their brains form connections, and thus mould their subsequent individual development.

Using ultrasound techniques, researchers were able to examine the nature of prenatal differences in fraternal twins by measuring each baby's independent patterns of movements and responses to stimuli. They found that quite often one twin was more active, reacted to a sudden stimulus with a faster heart rate or more vigorous kicking, or sucked her thumb more often than the other, more passive twin. Interestingly, these subtle differences persisted after birth, and follow-up studies of the twins at age four demonstrated similar characteristics to those observed in the womb.

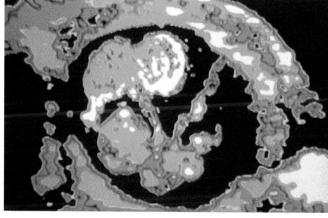

So far, no studies have examined prenatal differences in identical twins. But we can presume that although they at first have almost identical brains as a result of shared genes – and may thus show much more similar reactions to fraternal twins in utero – even the tiniest difference in the way each experiences her environment (before *and* after birth) will lead to the development of individual personalities. Scientists are thus increasingly beginning to conclude that nature (the genes a person is endowed with) and nurture (the environment and a person's particular life experiences, in and out of the womb) play *equally* vital, though different, roles in shaping an individual's personality and intellectual and physical development. Even identical twins never end up absolutely identical in personality or looks. A love of music, for example, may cause one twin to develop denser connections in certain areas of her brain, while a love of sport may encourage the other to develop a different body shape from that of her 'identical' twin sister.

Twins compete for nutrients and space as they develop together in utero. When one twin changes position, she forces the other to accommodate.

What else do I experience?

I woke up to a strange and unpleasant sensation today. Mum's voice sounded different, which made me feel distressed. Everything around me tightened, and I couldn't get back to sleep. What's happening out there?

As you become increasingly attuned to your environment, you will begin to react to changes in your mother's mood. What you experienced this morning was your mum's stress. But don't fret unduly. Occasional ups and downs are a normal part of life, and you are learning an invaluable fact of life: that the outside world doesn't always run as smoothly as your own diminutive world inside the womb.

FIRST FEELINGS As the foetus develops and becomes increasingly attuned to her environment, she begins to react to changes in her mother's mood. If the mother is unhappy, the tone of her voice, the level of tension that she experiences and the chemicals released by her body in response to mood alterations all signal to the unborn baby that something is not quite right. We often think of unhappiness, anger or euphoria as purely emotional states, overlooking the fact that these emotions also result in complex physical reactions. Think how exhausted you can feel after a good cry, for example, or after a particularly heated argument. Emotions can trigger a whole range of chemical responses: if you experience fear, your body reacts with a rush of adrenaline; when you are elated, endorphins are released in your body – thus proving the saying, 'Laughter is the best medicine!' In a pregnant woman, such substances are released into her bloodstream and are then carried around her body to the blood-rich placenta, where they pass into her baby's circulation. The foetus will then have a similar reaction to that of her mother: she will experience a sense of calm and contentment when her mother's endorphin levels rise or a quickened heart rate when maternal adrenaline levels increase.

With this in mind, it isn't surprising that a foetus is affected by her mother's emotional states. Maternal stress may cause the foetus to become agitated: the baby learns to associate her own increased agitation (for example, her quicker heartbeat, more kicking) with the sounds she is hearing

Not in front of the children

It is easy to remember not to argue when children or babies are in earshot, but we often forget that a little one inside also can be affected by our moments of stress.

Whenever possible, therefore, try to avoid serious arguments and upsets in the last months of pregnancy. If a heated

exchange does take place, or you become tearful or angry for any reason, take time out afterwards and concentrate on being calm and relaxed. Listen to music, read a good novel, put your feet up, have a massage – anything to soothe the tension. Your baby will be grateful for the return to a peaceful environment!

at that time, such as the mother's emotional voice, and perhaps her mother's jerky movements. Research so far has shown that a foetus's reactions to her mother's voice increase dramatically when her mother is experiencing high levels of tension. The unborn baby may become increasingly agitated in response to arguments or upsets, and it may take longer for her to settle down again. The level of stress experienced by the mother can also affect the regularity of her unborn baby's sleeping patterns.

Psychologists are becoming more and more interested in the long-term effects these prenatal experiences might have on a baby's postnatal behaviour. For example, studies have shown that higher foetal heart rates and greater motor activity predicted some aspects of newborn temperament such as irritability. But it is impossible to establish the exact extent to which stress-related experiences in the womb affect a baby's postnatal behaviour because other factors, such as the way mothers react to their babies at birth, obviously have an impact on newborn behaviour as well. Mothers who have been stressed throughout their pregnancies may continue to experience high levels of stress after the birth and communicate this to their babies.

Although negative early experiences such as maternal stress can be unpleasant for the unborn baby, they obviously can't be avoided altogether. In fact, provided they are balanced with happy and content emotions, they may play an important part in teaching the foetus something about how humans communicate different emotions, which is good preparation for life in the outside world. What is important is that after an argument, or indeed any stressful episode, a pregnant woman purposefully takes time out to calm down and have positive thoughts.

When pregnant women exercise, their regular movements, the release of endorphins into their circulation, and the increased oxygen in the blood probably give their babies a high as well.

THE SENSE OF VISION As early as 25 weeks, when the eyelids become unsealed, the foetus starts to blink. Her eyelids open and close in the dark as though she were practising for later visual stimulation in the outside world, after birth. At around 33 weeks' gestation, your baby becomes sensitive to changes in luminosity. A very bright light can penetrate the skin of the pregnant belly and filter through the wall of the uterus, changing the appearance of a baby's surroundings. It's a little like what we 'see' when we keep our eyes closed and turn from the dark to face a light: our eyelids take on a brighter shade. This change in brightness offers a new experience to your unborn baby and she may react by becoming

The strangest thing happened the other day. I was happily swimming around when suddenly, from one minute to the next, the walls around me got brighter with a strange glow. I kicked my legs to get some attention, but nothing happened. What is it that I saw?

What you noticed was light penetrating the wall of the uterus. Unfortunately, there isn't all that much for you to look at in there, so you spend much of your time with your eyes closed, using your other senses to keep you entertained. This early experience of light shows that your vision is already functioning even in the darkness of the womb.

more active as her heartbeat increases. But, although babies can already move their eyes from side to side in utero, they are not 'seeing' in the way we do: they are simply reacting to a change in the glow that illuminates the womb. They will only begin to see shapes and forms after birth.

Why do I spend so much time asleep? It seems an awful waste of time. I'd much rather concentrate on moving and growing, so that I can make my big entrance into this exciting world you keep talking about.

In the womb, you do spend most of your time sleeping, but that's not to say that you're inactive. While you sleep, your brain is busy working away, your body twitches and your eyes respond with little reflex movements. This is called 'rapid eye movement' or 'active sleep', a type of sleep associated with dreaming. You also have periods of quiet, deep sleep, but none of your resting time is wasted. Even while you sleep, you are continually developing, growing and preparing yourself for your birth day.

HOW BABIES SPEND THEIR TIME IN UTERO

Sleep patterns are established early during prenatal development and are not as easily disrupted as you might think. Generally, these patterns establish themselves quite independently of the mother's own daily and nightly schedule, and remain remarkably stable during the last three months or trimester. Pregnant women often become aware of the resting/waking rhythms of their unborn babies, and commonly report that their foetuses become most active just at the moment when they themselves are about to fall asleep! This is partly because the mother's motion when walking will to some degree reduce the baby's movements. It is also likely that the movements of the foetus are simply more noticeable at this time because the mother is taking a break and not moving herself.

Interacting with your unborn baby

When you're taking a rest and enjoying the final days with your soon-to-be-born child, try shining a spotlight close to the skin of your belly. You may feel changes in your baby's movements as she senses the light change and responds with active kicking. Then take it away and feel your baby slowly return to rest. Although this doesn't always happen (your baby may be sleeping), the game can be very rewarding as you get to experience a real interaction taking place between the two of you.

Another game parents can play with their unborn baby is to experiment with changes in pressure on the mother's belly. The foetus is very sensitive to alter-

ations in the dimensions of the uterine environment. In the late stages of pregnancy, the baby becomes increasingly restricted in her movements as the space available in the womb diminishes. Resting a book casually on your belly may not seem a big event to you, but you may get some objection from your baby as she becomes even more squashed. Such a small change in pressure is not harmful to the foetus, and may elicit vigorous pushing. The same thing can happen when someone asks to feel the baby kicking. The pressure from the hands placed right above your baby may result in some reciprocal action. Of course, more severe impacts on the womb must be avoided, as these could be harmful to the baby.

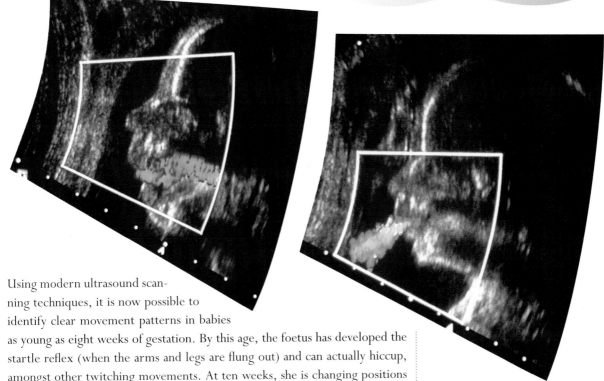

Using modern ultrasound scanning techniques, it is now possible to
identify clear movement patterns in babies
as young as eight weeks of gestation. By this age, the foetus has developed the
startle reflex (when the arms and legs are flung out) and can actually hiccup,
amongst other twitching movements. At ten weeks, she is changing positions
frequently by rotating her body, stretching, and moving her head, arms and
legs together. Breathing-type movements can also be seen, although these
occur every two or three seconds only. They represent a weaker version of the
stronger gulping action that develops around the eighteenth week.

By the time a baby reaches the second trimester, she will remain in one
position for greater lengths of time, content to float quietly, sucking her
thumb or hanging on to the umbilical cord. Her lungs are now developing fast.
Every second, they expand and retract, taking in amniotic fluid instead of air,
in preparation for breathing outside the womb. At this stage, these breathing
movements don't actually contribute to keeping the baby alive, as all the
oxygen she needs is carried to her in the blood, but they are vital for strengthening the lungs before birth. Breathing difficulties are one of the greatest problems faced by premature babies because their immature lungs are not always
ready to cope with the difficult transition from amniotic fluid to air.

By the third trimester, the foetus has very stable movement patterns,
including regular periods of sleep – during which her heartbeat slows down –
punctuated by briefer periods of activity. A significant proportion of her
movements now represents specific responses to sound, touch, changes in
light and other sensations. Although foetal rhythms are not necessarily
structured around the mother's day–night cycle, by now the foetus has also
established her own routines over a twenty-four-hour period.

*Amongst other intrauterine
activities, babies begin to practise breathing to strengthen
their lungs long before they are
needed for survival in the
outside world. These two scans
show a baby breathing in
amniotic fluid (shown in blue)
and exhaling it moments
later (orange).*

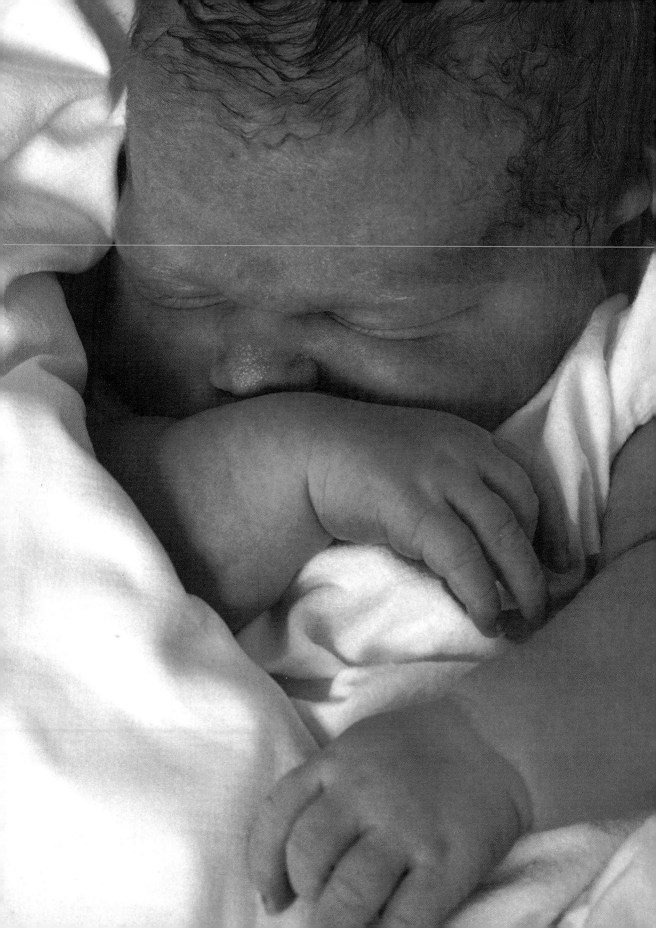

Being Born

When they are ready, babies plan the timing of their arrival into the outside world. However painful labour may be for the mother and her birthing partner, the stress is rapidly forgotten when the tiny newborn is placed in his parents' arms. A miracle has taken place. Within seconds of the birth, you'll probably feel a rush of love and protection for this little creature, although such feelings may momentarily dwindle a few days later when your baby has been crying non-stop for hours! Such swings of emotion towards your newborn are perfectly normal.

Scientists know a lot about labour, but we still do not know precisely what the infant himself experiences. Maybe we never will. All we can do is guess at the pain or discomfort he may feel and measure the various physiological changes taking place in his body. A newborn baby isn't usually very pretty. He may come out red-faced, wrinkled like an elderly man, or with his head very misshapen due to being compressed when passing through the birth canal. When his head emerges, and even before his body is fully pushed out, you'll see him blink from the bright lights of the delivery room and start to survey his surroundings, showing few signs of his exhausting journey into the outside world. In the meantime mum falls back on to the pillow in total exhaustion, and dad sighs with great relief that it's all over! But whatever your baby looks like and however tired you are, your newborn is probably the most beautiful sight you have ever seen.

From the moment of birth, your baby's brain is working overtime and already functions better than the smartest of computers! The pink, spongy brain mass within his skull looks wrinkled, a bit like a walnut, because of the way its layers are densely folded, one on top of the other. If we were to iron flat all the layers of the brain, the resulting surface would be almost the size of a football pitch! Each layer contains hundreds of millions of cells connected to each other and to cells in the various parts of the body, a little like the electrical system running through your house.

The cells in the brain are called neurons and come in different shapes and sizes. They look a bit like ferns or tree-like structures, with branches at the top called dendrites (which mainly receive messages from other neurons), and at the bottom trunk- or root-like structures called axons (which send messages to other neurons). Neurons can fire several hundred times per second, so when we recall that the brain contains some ten billion cells, the activity in the brain is literally mind-boggling! Between the dendrite of one neuron and the axon of another is a gap, technically known as a synapse. In this gap, electrical impulses are converted into chemical reactions. All sorts of chemicals, or neurotransmitters as they're called, pass through the synapses to link neurons to each other, forming an amazingly intricate network. A sheaf of a fatty substance known as myelin covers the axon, rather like electrical

insulation tape, and makes brain waves flow more efficiently between neurons. The process of myelination is not complete at birth and continues during the early years of life. Throughout development, and at every opportunity they have when processing new stimuli, neurons reach out to each other to form new connections and make your infant's brain increasingly complex. Your infant's brain is like a huge international telephone exchange, picking up new subscribers and new territories every second. No wonder your baby needs to sleep so much.

· ·

The brain is divided into two major parts: the cortex and the subcortex (which, from an evolutionary point of view, is the older part of the brain). The more primitive regions, which include the brain stem that controls heartbeat and breathing, are almost fully wired at birth. In the early weeks of life the subcortical regions are the most active; these govern reflexes. Other parts of the brain, particularly the cortex which is responsible for language, thinking, intricate movement and problem solving, only form their complex network of connections once the baby experiences the world outside. This is why it is so important to make sure that your baby is stimulated by new sounds, shapes, colours, textures, voices, music and moving objects.

· ·

During the early days after birth, your infant's brain will produce trillions of connections between neurons in most areas of the brain, far more than are actually needed. Subsequently a process of pruning will take place as the brain comes to realise which connections are important and which can be dispensed with. Infants' brains quadruple in volume between birth and adulthood, and most of this growth takes place during the first year, when babies learn more than at any other time of their lives.

What's it like being born?

I'm not sure I'm going to fit in here much longer, so I'm all packed and ready to leave. But I can't find the way out, or any buttons to press. Am I going to be stuck here? How do I tell mum it's time to let me come out?

When the time has come for you to pop out into the world, your body will give a special signal to your mum's body, and the mechanisms that induce your birth will automatically be set off. You don't need to push any buttons: just get yourself in the right position and be patient. It can be a long and bumpy ride!

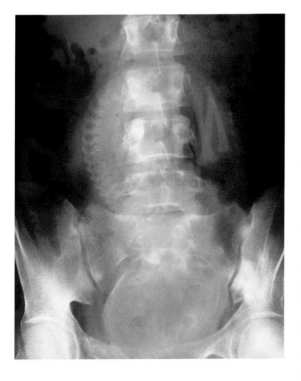

The full-term baby in this x-ray has dropped into the engaged position, his head pressing into his mother's pelvic cavity ready to make the short yet arduous journey to the outside world.

HOW BABIES SET THEIR OWN BIRTH DATES

To some extent, the precise triggers of childbirth remain a mystery to scientists. By the thirty-sixth week, the baby is so big that he won't be able to turn around and change positions again before birth. But he remains inside because the next four weeks of pregnancy are crucial for preparing him for life outside the womb. This is the time when his heart and lungs mature and gain strength. Fat tissues are also laid down rapidly under the skin to insulate him when he leaves the constant warmth of his mother's body; this is what gives babies the characteristic chubby look with which they are born.

The brain is also developing very actively during these last few weeks of preparation, and will be protected from damage during birth by the special structure of the skull. By the end of gestation, the separate plates of bone that make up the baby's skull are still not fused. During labour, the strong contractions squeeze the baby's head as he manoeuvres down the tight canal and through his mother's pelvic opening. The flexible skull plates can move and overlap one another to accommodate all this pressure, preventing the skull itself from being crushed and ensuring that no harm comes to vital brain tissue.

Once the baby's head engages (that is, his head settles down against his mother's pelvis), the scene is set for delivery. The minor contractions mothers may have been experiencing over the last few months get stronger as the womb prepares itself for the formidable task ahead. There is some evidence that foetal adrenal glands (which produce the hormone, adrenaline) play a leading role in triggering birth, which is why babies are said to set their own birth date. However, the onset of labour also involves a whole range of other factors. The mother's body responds to foetal adrenaline by secreting its own cocktail of hormones into her bloodstream. These are responsible for initiating the contraction activity in the muscles of her uterus and the simultaneous dilation of her cervix.

The process of giving birth is now in Nature's hands. But parents can have a huge impact on how it proceeds. Being prepared physically and mentally will help both the mother and her birthing partner become attuned to the changing demands of labour. No matter how many times a parent, doctor or midwife have experienced labour, each birth is unique and magical.

THE BIRTH EXPERIENCE Well before the delivery itself, parents can read books and attend antenatal classes to learn about the details of the different stages of labour. So, although it is impossible for expectant mothers and fathers to imagine what labour will really be like until it actually happens, they at least know what to expect. By contrast, the baby has no idea what he's in for. His body simply sends an early warning signal that something very new is about to happen. This occurs even before the mother herself is aware of her first contractions. Nonetheless, the foetus will have been preparing for this big day for quite some time – getting into position and gradually slipping down so that his head engages. Yet it is only at the onset of labour, when hormone levels rise, that everything around the womb is set into motion. This is the moment everyone has been waiting for.

Why can I hear everyone shouting 'Push! Push?' Hold on, I seem to be on the move! Wow, what a tight squeeze, I don't think I'm going to fit down this tunnel. Is this going to hurt me, Mum?

We don't know if it's going to hurt, because none of us can remember what it was like being born. We can only guess what you experience as you make your way down the birth canal and out into the open arms of mum and dad. You must have felt many changes around you when the amniotic liquid drained away and the walls of the uterus started to contract. We have machines that can monitor your heartbeat, but beyond that your birth remains your own little secret.

Of course, the baby will have become quite accustomed to the intermittent hardening of the uterine muscles that occurs from slight contractions throughout pregnancy. But these are nothing in comparison to the strength of the contractions he will experience as labour gets going. First, the dilation of the cervix causes the membranes containing the amniotic fluid to rupture, or medical staff may intervene to break the bag of waters. The baby's environment changes rapidly thanks to the reduced fluid around his body and the increasingly strong pressure exerted by the muscles around the womb. These push him further and further down the birth canal.

While the journey from the comfort of the womb to a new life in the outside world is only a few inches long, it often takes hours. Like the mother, the baby experiences periods of rest interspersed by moments of intense activity and, with each new contraction, it is probable that the infant experiences some discomfort. From the moment the amniotic liquid leaks out of the uterus, the uterine walls begin to close in and make contact with his skin. We can presume the baby, no longer 'floating' in fluid, feels some change, if not actual pain. However, there is still some fluid left around the baby, which flows

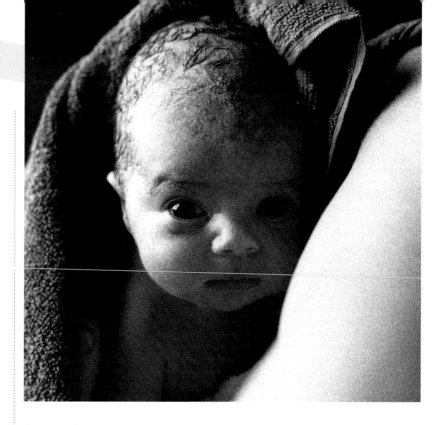

Now cleaned and wrapped in a towel to keep her warm, this baby girl is fully alert – despite having squeezed out from her mother's narrow birth canal only minutes earlier.

down the birth canal to moisten it. Further lubrication is provided by a waxy substance known as vernix, which has been protecting the surface of the baby's skin during his prolonged exposure to the amniotic liquid in the womb.

We can be pretty sure that birth is a dramatic experience for a baby, but does it hurt? The delivery team can assess the level of stress experienced by the baby by monitoring his heart rate, but it is difficult to determine the extent to which he actually feels pain. We do know, however, that newborns *react* to pain and instinctively withdraw from an unpleasant stimulus such as a pin-prick, even though the nerves in their skin are not as sensitive as ours. Research also indicates that sensitivity to pain increases with age. So, a five-day-old infant can feel more pain than an hour-old baby. But how newborns actually *experience* pain or the sensations of being squashed down the narrow birth canal remain a mystery.

It is thought that the sudden surge of adrenaline, the hormone that flows through the newborn's system throughout labour, shields him from discomfort. A baby's adrenaline level is twice that of his mother during labour, who is herself in a highly agitated state. This hormone not only helps the baby cope with birth, it also plays an important role in stimulating the infant's organs (which, don't forget, have been dormant until now) as he takes his first gulp of air and the umbilical cord is cut. This is the moment when, for the first time, the baby's body has to fend for itself. The high levels of adrenaline are maintained for some two hours after the birth, after which they finally normalise and the baby is able to sleep off the exhausting ordeal.

FIRST IMPRESSIONS OF THE OUTSIDE WORLD After the comfort of floating in the warmth of the amniotic liquid, the cool air of the delivery room is a shock to the baby's already very alert senses. The hustle and bustle, and the excitement and emotion that surround this event don't go unnoticed by the little person held firmly in the midwife's caring hands. Newborns are more alert during the moments following birth than at any time over the next few days. Your baby has been propelled into a world in which he very quickly has to learn how to control the people around him, so that they supply him with all the warmth, food, care and comfort he needs to survive.

Babies open their eyes almost immediately after birth, usually as they start to breathe. Unlike the senses of hearing and touch, up to now a baby's vision has not been well exercised, for although a foetus regularly opens and closes his eyes, the womb does not offer a very stimulating environment visually. It's too dark in there. Now, as baby begins his life in the outside world, he is suddenly bombarded with a multitude of faces, objects, colours, contours, shapes and sizes. These sights can be quite overwhelming, even though, at this stage, he can only focus up to 20–25 cm (8–10 inches) away. This is exactly the distance between the feeding infant's eyes and his

I really don't know what to make of the outside world! I feel completely overwhelmed because everything's happening at once. I'm seeing, hearing and feeling so many new things, and none of them make any sense. Will I ever be able to cope with all these new sensations?

Your first taste of life outside the womb is dazzling and bewildering. All your senses are suddenly bombarded with new information. The air feels cold, and you are surrounded by strange smells, sounds, things and people. Right now, your body and mind are in a hyper-alert state and your experiences are jumbled. But don't worry, things will soon fall into place. Mum and dad are probably just as overwhelmed as you at the moment. They, too, have a lot to learn!

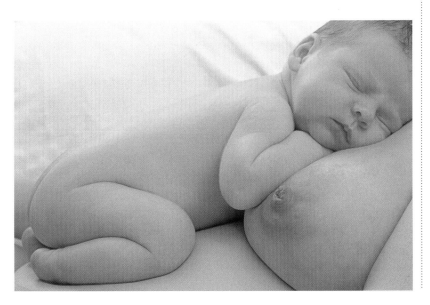

Nestled on mum's breast, where he can hear the comforting sound of his mother's heartbeat, this newborn baby sleeps off the exhausting experience of birth.

Welcoming your baby

The outside world can be very disorientating to a new baby, but there are a number of things you can do to help him adjust and feel loved and secure. For example, you may think that because your baby doesn't yet speak or understand language, there's no point speaking to him. But actually you can start a dialogue with your baby from the moment he's born. Don't forget he's spent the last three months listening in to your conversations and getting to know the patterns of your voice and those around you. Once cradled in your arms, he will quickly begin to recognise the voices he used to hear in the womb. You may notice him copying your facial expressions as well. Be sure to hold him to your skin so he can learn your special smell. This early communication is extremely important, not only to help you both form a unique bond but also to help your baby orient himself in his bewildering new environment. Lying on your chest he will be calmed by the familiar sound of your heartbeat, which has lulled him to sleep for the past few months. In a few weeks' time, if you coo to him, he may even attempt to respond with his own little sounds. And if you suddenly speak with an excited voice, he may notice your mood change and respond by kicking more vigorously.

mother's face. So a baby can recognise the general shape of his mother's face very early. As his sight is blurred beyond this distance, he cannot make out any details, but he will still be fascinated by anything moving in the background. Newborns cannot yet follow movement smoothly because their eyes can only make jerky attempts to keep up with the things that move across their fields of vision. The ability to bring objects into focus and to make sense of their size, depth and distance takes years to develop (see also pages 162–5).

The sounds that fill the delivery room also provide instant stimulation for the new baby. Particularly intriguing is his mother's voice, which filtered through the amniotic liquid to him so many times before. Now, out in the open, it sounds different but he can still recognise its familiar sound patterns (see pages 17–19). More interesting still is the sound of his own voice when he utters his first cry. Sometimes the midwife has to clear mucus from the newborn's air passages by suction, so parents won't hear their baby cry until then.

As he takes in the air around him, new smells fill his nostrils. A newborn's sense of smell is extremely well developed, perhaps to make up for his blurry vision. Once he has learned an individual smell, he can use it to locate mum or dad, for example, by turning his head in the direction of the familiar odour. This is one of the reasons parents are encouraged to make skin-to-skin contact with their newborns as often as possible – such cuddling not only enhances bonding and comfort, but also allows the infant to get to know his parents' particular smells.

How does my body cope on its own?

BREATHING ALONE The transition from the womb to the outside world results in a number of significant changes in the way the infant's organs function, placing new demands on the body as a whole. During intrauterine life, for example, foetal blood circulation is such that most of the oxygen is sent to the upper half of the body and, most importantly, to the brain. Blood circulating in the lower half of the body contains much less oxygen. In a sense, the upper body is given priority. Special bypasses ensure this continues right up to birth. From the moment the infant begins breathing alone, however, his blood circulation changes so these bypasses cease to operate. As the mother no longer provides the baby with oxygen, the baby's body must henceforth learn to extract it from the air that will now fill his lungs. His blood circulation stops prioritising certain parts of the body, but rather ensures that enough oxygen is made available throughout the body to cope with life outside the womb.

During intrauterine life, the lungs are filled with amniotic liquid. Most of this is expelled during labour, when contractions press down on the baby's chest, but just to be certain that the airways are clear, the newborn is generally dangled upside down and given a gentle massage. This makes him cry and, together with the effect of cold air on his skin for the first time, causes messages to be sent to the brain to start up regular breathing movements.

Even the lungs of full-term infants are not completely developed, so breathing can be a little erratic at first. This is because some of the little sacs inside the lungs, which fill with air at each breath, have not yet opened. Becoming fully expert at the breathing business can take up to six months, during which some fundamental reorganisations of the respiratory system take place. This is why respiratory diseases and cot death are more common in young babies.

Hmm, I like having my skin rubbed like this. Do you always get a free massage when you come out of the womb, or does this rubbing have a special purpose?

The massage is to stimulate your breathing, so that you take air into your lungs for the first time. Until now, mum's been breathing for both of you. Your lungs were busy getting strong in preparation for today, but they were full of fluid and didn't actually keep you alive. This has all changed now. The umbilical cord has been cut and you need to get oxygen into your body from the air around you. Don't worry, though. Breathing comes naturally and once you're used to it you won't even notice you're doing it.

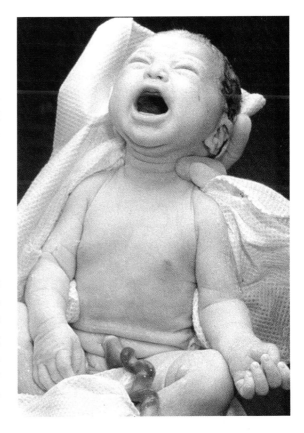

Infants are born swimmers. Gently lowered into warm water, this young baby can propel herself forwards and is prevented from drowning by a special valve that closes the tract between her mouth and lungs. Sadly, this skill doesn't last beyond four to six months of age.

Sometimes babies show very brief periodic cessation of breathing. Unless this happens frequently and for longer than ten seconds, it is usually just part of the process of learning to breathe naturally. However, if it does occur, it is always best to tell your doctor, who can then decide whether your baby's breathing needs to be monitored.

During the early months of life, the infant's respiratory system is not the same as that of older infants. In fact, there is a period when the newborn can swim without filling his lungs and drowning. This is because, until the voice box starts to descend between four and six months of age, a valve automatically shuts off the passage between the mouth and lungs when the baby is under water. It's a little like returning to the amniotic fluid inside the womb. (Of course, parents should never try swimming with their young infants without expert supervision.)

I'm only a few hours old, and I already have all these clever instincts. I feel compelled to grab your finger when you touch my palm, and to walk when you hold me upright over a table. Am I something of a genius?

Unfortunately these instincts aren't signs of intelligence because reflexes are automatic. Breathing is just one of these. Other reflexes, like grasping and walking, also help you cope with your new environment. But it won't be long before you begin to control these involuntary reactions and replace them with the responses you've learned.

NEWBORN REFLEXES Babies are born fully dependent on us for their physical and emotional wellbeing. Having said that, a series of reflexes helps them cope with life outside the womb. An example is the grasping reflex, whereby the newborn automatically tightens his fingers around an object that touches the palm of his hand. This differs from reaching and grabbing for an object because it is involuntary. Unfortunately for parents who tend to lose chunks of hair in the process, letting go is not part of the grasping reflex. The ability to release tightly gripped objects has to be learned – though often with some reluctance, it seems!

In contrast to, say, the sucking reflex, the early grasping reflex doesn't really contribute to the newborn's survival. He doesn't need it to feed or to hold on to a support, as adults supply all he requires. So what is it for? Well, we can trace the evolutionary origins of the grasping reflex by looking at the behaviour of newborn primates, our ancestral cousins. From the moment they are born, baby monkeys and apes depend on the grasping ability to hold tightly on to their mothers' bodies as they move around. Without this, a mother and baby would become separated. Human babies need not hang on to their mothers themselves as bipedalism means that the mother's hands are free to hold the infant, leaving *his* hands idle. It may well be, therefore, that in humans the original function of the grasping reflex has now been replaced by another role – to promote the baby's tactile exploration of the world. Recall that in the womb, the foetus grasped the umbilical cord whenever it brushed against his hand, thereby stimulating his sense of touch (*see page 22*). Such early reflexes are important ways with which the baby comes to know the world.

Another reflex parents may notice occurs either in response to the baby's head dropping back, or to startling sounds or sensations. This is the Moro reflex. The infant reacts by outstretching his arms and legs momentarily before letting them gradually fall back together. It serves to arouse the baby in response to a sudden stimulus that might represent danger. But perhaps the most astonishing reflex of all is the walking reflex, which is something of an enigma to scientists. If held under their arms in an upright position touching a flat surface, infants automatically lift one leg after another in a coordinated walking action. This response fades a few weeks after birth, in part because it is not being exercised as the baby's muscles are too weak to allow him to stand, and in part because he is gaining voluntary control over his leg movements. Present at birth, this reflex may not seem directly connected to the process of learning to walk a year later, but in fact practising the reflex very early on may set up a template for walking in the memory stores of the brain. As the stepping action is repeated in sequences, links form between the cells in the area

Because newborns have so little voluntary control over their bodies, reflexes are crucial for their survival. (Left) The grasping reflex: when something touches a baby's palm, she will automatically clench her fingers. (Right) If a baby's head drops back suddenly, the baby will throw out her arms and legs, demonstrating the Moro reflex.

If you hold your new baby upright with his feet touching a flat surface, he will move his legs in a walking action.

of the brain responsible for subsequent walking. A schematic system is thus established which may be called upon later to guide the baby's first steps when he is strong enough to support his own weight.

Doctors can use reflexes to assess a newborn's development (the Apgar test performed just after birth, for example, consists of assessing the baby's reflexes). The lack of strong reflexes may indicate problems that occurred in utero or during birth. However, testing reflexes is not always straightforward. The baby's level of alertness at the time of testing can have a significant effect on the results. Parents may become a little concerned if they are not getting the response they expect; but try to remember that being tired or distracted, or having just woken or been fed, can all influence a baby's reactions. Under the right conditions, marvelling at your newborn's abilities can be a lot of fun.

We often take our own reflexes for granted, forgetting that many of them actually stay with us from birth and play an important role in the functioning and protection of our bodies. The blinking reflex, for example, not only keeps our eyes moist, but also protects the corneas from harmful light and the eyes in general from approaching objects. Your newborn will automatically close his eyes if something makes contact with the bridge of his nose, if he is startled by a bright light or loud noise, or if he feels a rush of air on his face.

The role of reflexes is not always obvious. Some may simply be leftovers from our evolutionary past or from the demands of life in the womb. Others, such as breathing, are crucial for survival. Others still, such as the rooting and sucking reflexes discussed overleaf, serve an immediate though short-lived role, helping the infant cope with the new challenges of life in the outside world. Many of the newborn's reflexes, however, will later have to be unlearned or overcome as the infant learns to control his own behaviour.

A BABY'S BRAIN: BORN TO LEARN

From the moment of birth, the newborn's brain is poised for an explosion of learning. This is the period when the infant will learn more than at any other time in his life, and one during which he actually structures his own brain as a result of the multitude of experiences he encounters. But even prior to birth, the infant's brain is very active. Scientists have now documented waves of spontaneous rhythmic firing of cells in various parts of the brain during foetal life.

The brain can be divided into two major parts: the subcortex and the cortex. The basic six-layer structure of the different regions of cortex is already formed at birth. However, it is not until after birth, when the newborn is bombarded with sensations from the outside world, that the complex network of micro-connections within and between different areas of the cortex rapidly develop. By contrast, the pathways of the subcortex and the brain stem, which are the more primitive and oldest parts of the brain from an evolutionary point of view, are formed during foetal life. It is these that govern the set of reflexes the newborn displays during the first few weeks of life, as well as crucial functions like breathing and heartbeat. From the moment of birth, the rate at which cells in the cortex transmit and receive messages, in the form of bursts of electrical impulses, is increased dramatically. This heralds the gradual onset of voluntary action and a time when stimulation from the outside world is crucial to the developing brain.

With the advent of a non-invasive technique called Event Related Potentials or ERPs, scientists can now measure the electrical activity of the brains of even tiny infants, and compare reflexes

As babies become toddlers, the pathways in the brain become increasingly specialised, thanks in large part to a stimulating environment.

in the subcortex to the more complex processes of the cortex. ERPs involve gently placing a hairnet containing up to 64 sensors on the infant's head. Nothing enters the infant's brain: the net just records the electrical activity produced naturally. You might compare ERPs to taking your infant's temperature, in that the thermometer simply records changes in body temperature but itself has no effect on his body. ERPs allow researchers to trace the gradual specialisation of the infant brain into pathways that will govern, for example, the ability to recognise faces or discriminate speech sounds, and various forms of motor coordination. Although initially the infant may activate several pathways in the brain when processing particular kinds of stimuli, the brain will be progressively fine-tuned, with some of these pathways being pruned and the more active ones retained. The same applies to reflexes. With time, those reflexes that weaken during infancy will show far less activity in the brain than those that, like the blinking reflex, we retain throughout life.

Shortly after I was born, mum held me very close. It was amazing! The moment I felt something touch the side of my face, I could not stop my head from turning towards it nor my mouth from opening to suck. What is this wonderful new experience?

This was your first experience of being fed. Your reflexes guided you towards the nipple and prompted you to suck hard so as to draw liquid. Although the main purpose of this is to feed you and provide your body with energy, mealtimes are also important for another reason: they help you build a trusting relationship with your parents. You may find feeding a bit tricky at first as it involves juggling several different reflexes simultaneously, but you'll improve daily.

THE FIRST FEED During the twenty-four hours after birth, your baby will have his first meal. Whether or not mothers decide to breast-feed, the milk-producing glands in their breasts will have been set to work by the activities of labour. The instant the baby begins to suck, hormones cause the release of milk from the glands into the nipples. During the first 72 hours or so after delivery, the breasts produce a thin, watery fluid called colostrum. This is a unique liquid containing a whole range of antibodies, proteins and minerals. It boosts the newborn's immune system, providing him with the means to fight off infection. This is why mothers are encouraged to breast-feed whenever possible. After a few days, the mother starts to produce milk which gradually thickens, containing more fat and protein which are so vital for the baby's growth.

Infants don't generally feel hunger immediately after birth. In fact – because of all the energy they exerted during labour and their alertness to their new surroundings once it's all over – food is probably the last thing on their minds! Yet newborns are equipped with a strong instinct to feed. The rooting reflex is responsible for orienting the baby's mouth towards a nipple (breast or bottle) when it's brushed against the side of the mouth or the cheek. The sucking reflex then takes over, prompting the baby to take the nipple into his mouth and suck. A mouthful of milk in turn triggers the swallowing reflex.

It is all too easy to forget how complicated feeding is. The different reflexes must be well-coordinated if it's going to work out successfully. Some babies find getting to grips with mealtimes easier than others, and parents may have to be patient if their little one is coughing and spluttering a little at first. Infants usually become expert at feeding after about three weeks, but some

One of the most important instincts, the rooting reflex helps your baby start feeding. Brush a finger or nipple against his cheek, and he will turn towards it, opening his mouth.

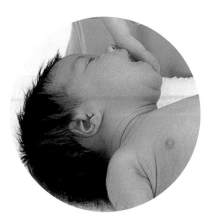

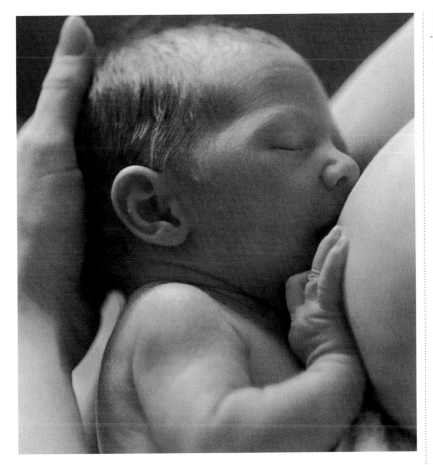

The physical closeness of breast-feeding helps to develop the bond between a mother and her newborn baby.

take longer. If repetitive sucking doesn't occur immediately, this can be assisted by moving the nipple around the edges of the baby's mouth and gently in and out. With lots of practice, the baby becomes better not only at latching on properly, but also at sucking. He learns about the shape of the nipple, the strength of pull needed to produce the right amount of milk, and how to alert mum that it's time for another feed. Amusingly, the mother's body becomes so attuned to her baby's cries for food that sometimes even another baby's tears can make her milk start to flow.

The infant's very first meal is an important experience for both parent and child. It is one of those private moments when bonding is established. We know that babies respond better to their mother's voice if she has been actively communicating with eye contact, words and strokes during feeding. A baby may even stop sucking momentarily to attend intently to his mother's encouragements. As the baby responds with a contented look, so his mother initiates further exchanges, and an increasingly deep bond is established.

Relating to Myself and Others

How do infants come to understand that they are individuals with bodies, minds and emotions of their own, and at the same time part of a social world? Two processes — getting to know oneself and forming relationships with parents, siblings and others outside the family — develop in parallel during early infancy and beyond.

Self-awareness is a lengthy process that starts with the infant's discovery of how to control her own body parts. Such purposeful movements begin around two months, and your baby may spend hours playing with her hands and fingers, holding on to her feet, opening and closing her mouth and eyes. If you see her chewing her feet, it doesn't mean she is hungry! Rather, she is investigating how that part of her body feels.

Becoming self-aware and learning to be an individual member of the social world also involves learning about gender. It doesn't matter how many dolls you buy your baby son or trains you offer your daughter, your child will probably turn out to be as conventional as the others, at least in the early years. Gender-related play occurs in almost all children, not only as a result of peer pressure in play groups, but also from subtle clues you yourself unwittingly give your child (adults simply seem to behave differently towards boys and girls.) Your infant will pick up on these signs and build her own identity accordingly.

It may seem paradoxical to say that close bonding with parents also helps the infant to become self-aware and a separate, independent individual. Yet the child who feels secure is far more likely to explore the world and her special place in it. Cuddles and reassurance encourage her to explore beyond the limits of her

environment and help her build trust in others. This all starts very early in the first year, when infants discover they are part of a family, be it a one-parent, two-parent or extended family. An infant should feel loved and cared for in a consistent way, from a parent or care-giver who responds sensitively to her reactions.

• •

As her social world progressively grows, the securely attached baby will also experience a couple of periods of fear of other people and fear of losing you. Technically these are called 'fear of strangers' and 'separation anxiety'. Both are perfectly normal reactions as your infant comes to realise her place in the social world and to distinguish between the stable and the passing relations in her life.

• •

How does your baby build up mental images of others? Initially babies learn about their social environment almost exclusively via their parents or care-givers. By the time your baby is born, she will already know your voice, having heard it so often in utero, but after birth she will also rapidly learn about your face and come to recognise you and other family members. She'll build up a mental image of each person from their face, gait, voice and smell, and with time she will react differently to each person, showing that she is not only becoming an individual in her own right but also individuating those around her.

During the second half of the first year, your baby will become less exclusively focused on her care-giver and start to seek the attention of others. But this is not always reciprocal. Indeed, one person who may not be pleased to see the arrival of the newborn is an older sister or brother. Imagine if you came home one evening and your husband said: 'You don't mind, do you Dear, if this adorable young lady moves in permanently with us, if she sleeps with us when she's upset, if you now have to share my attention with her, and if all our visitors say how cute she is!' This may capture roughly what the older sibling experiences as the newborn is brought home. Parents have to handle sibling rivalry cleverly, making sure that the older child is given special attention and allowed temporarily to regress to a baby himself.

Up to now, baby's interactions have been rather dependent in nature, with parents, care-givers and siblings being the dominant partner. But from now on the child starts to form increasingly equal relations with peers and others. This is in part due to the fact that she has begun to understand that other people have minds like hers. Now she doesn't only observe what they do, but also tries to work out what they think and feel. This process starts in infancy with simple activities such as following another's gaze, humourous acts like playing peek-a-boo, or trying to anticipate what a person will do next. As the child matures, the realisation that others have feelings enables her to display positive and negative behaviour. To deceive someone requires what psychologists refer to as a 'theory of mind'. But this also allows the child to show empathy towards another person's emotions, and to become a sympathetic member of her ever-expanding social world.

How do I get to know myself?

I seem to be quite a complicated piece of machinery. Every day I find a new part of my body that I didn't realise I had, and discover new ways of making these move and do interesting things. These wiggly toe things are my favourite – why do I spend so much time playing with them?

When you're lying on your back, looking for things to play with, your toes are always within reach. They provide you with hours of fun and help you discover how your skin feels, smells and tastes. Finding out about how your whole body works will take a long time. You'll gradually discover that you can control the different parts of your body, and this will give you the confidence to try new movements and positions. As you get to know your body, your brain progressively forms a map of how its parts are coordinated.

HOW BABIES LEARN ABOUT THEIR BODIES

Little is known about infants' knowledge of their own bodies. In the womb, the foetus discovers the feel of her own thumb, and may touch her feet or join hands. However, we cannot conclude that the foetus is already forming any sort of mental representation of what she looks like. This prenatal activity is reflex driven, occurring largely by chance. At birth, the so-called Babinsky reflex drives the infant to place her hand in her mouth, and within a few weeks you will notice your baby spending much of her time fascinated by the way her hands and feet look, taste and move. These body parts act as ready-made and constantly available playthings, entertaining her even when you are not around. At this stage, however, the learning process involves little more than the baby finding out about the many interesting *bits* she has and can move. It will be some months before she can coordinate her hands with any adroitness (*see pages 132–51*) or gains sufficient control over her legs to crawl or walk (*pages 108–31*). During the first few weeks of life, then, this series of discoveries serves to enable the baby's brain to form a sensory map of her body. A true sense of what her body looks like, and a basic understanding of what it can do as a whole system, will not emerge until your child begins to develop a self-concept, demonstrated by her changing reactions to her mirror image (*see overleaf*). Healthy bonding also requires the development of a self-concept – your baby needs to feel as close to you as possible without believing that you and she are one. Bonding is discussed in more detail on pages 55–8.

Discovering her own body is an important part of a baby's development, as it helps her gradually to distinguish herself from other people in general, and to gain control over her actions. Her sense of individuality, of gender, of independence and of self-control, are not only brought about through her

WHAT DO CHILDREN UNDERSTAND OF THEIR OWN BODIES?

It would be fascinating to be able to take a peek at the mental images a baby might have of her own body before she recognises her own reflection in the mirror for the first time. But before the emergence of language, it is difficult to devise ways of 'asking' just how much the baby does know. Some of the research techniques described on page 16 might be used. For instance, if the baby were repeatedly shown a correct drawing of the human body and then shown one with two heads, would she show surprise by looking longer at the strange picture? Or alternatively, given a choice between a 'tadpole drawing' (*see below*) and one with the arms and body added, would the young infant show a preference by sucking harder on a dummy? Such experiments might well reveal to what level of detail young babies mentally represent the human body.

The development of children's representation of the human body has in general been investigated through the examination of children's drawings of the human form. As early as two and a half, toddlers begin to draw people. These early scribbles usually consist of only the head and legs. Researchers call this the 'tadpole' representation of the human body. It isn't that toddlers see the body in this way – from early infancy babies can see what the human form is really like – it is just the way they conceptualise it when they first start drawing.

There are many different theories about why youngsters initially represent a person's entire body in this minimalist way. Some have suggested that it perhaps indicates that at this age a child's knowledge of the human body is incomplete. However, if asked to name the different parts of the body, toddlers regu-

When children first start drawing recognisable representations of human beings, they tend to produce what are known as 'tadpole' people: big round head-cum-body amalgamated into one, with legs (and sometimes arms) attached directly to the head.

larly identify the arms, tummy or hands. They can also successfully put together a simple puzzle of a person's head, torso, arms and legs. So why are only the head and legs represented in their early drawings? To answer that question, we must remember that drawing is a complicated task for the very young child. Movements of arms, hands and fingers have to be controlled and carefully coordinated, and the toddler must make the connection between moving a pencil with her hand and producing a trace on the paper. To further translate what she sees into a series of movements that will create a drawing is extremely tricky. Therefore, it is thought that when drawing a human, the young artist selects features that are both important and which, put together, give a balanced and well-proportioned representation in the simplest and most manageable way possible. Faces are very important to babies (*see pages 59–61*). Adding long legs to the head is the easiest way to give the head a 'body' – to give the drawing spatial realism. A third interpretation of the tadpole representation posits that the drawing is an abstract depiction of the human body. Early drawings of people are produced at a time when young children are engaging in active symbolic play, where a nest of pillows can represent a ship, or the underneath of a table can be a mysterious cave (*see pages 187–8*). One could therefore expect the same type of abstraction and imagination in drawing.

interaction with others, but are also influenced by the way she comes to know herself. Babies discover the different parts of their bodies through exploration and play. They should never be discouraged from doing so, even if it causes embarrassment to parents. Your child needs the freedom to find out about every aspect of her body – what each part does, feels, smells and tastes like – so that she can gradually build a picture of who and what she is. This exploration helps her learn about herself and encourages her to build a confident and unashamed attitude towards her body, her nakedness and the individual characteristics that make her unique. It also helps her learn about the world through her tactile senses, for example by putting objects in her mouth to explore their unique properties (known as 'mouthing': *see pages 167–8*).

That face in the mirror looks as confused as I do. Who is this person, and why does she copy everything I do?

What you're seeing in the mirror is your own reflection. That's why it smiles at you whenever you smile, reaches out towards you whenever you stretch your arm out to touch the mirror, and looks as bewildered as you do by all of this. You don't know what you look like when you're born. Your self-recognition develops gradually during your first year, and you'll spend a lot of time during the next few months studying your reflection, pulling faces, communicating with it and growing to love it.

ACQUIRING SELF-AWARENESS A baby's concept of self develops very gradually. It is a product of the interaction between the child and her physical and social environments. When babies are born, they don't make a clear distinction between themselves and the rest of their environment. In other words, they are not entirely sure where their own selves and bodies end and other people and objects begin. Clarifying this is part of the learning process.

Developing a sense of the self as a separate entity begins with the ability to situate oneself, or more specifically, one's body, within the immediate environment. At birth, the infant's actions are largely reflex-driven and involuntary. Day by day, the baby's brain learns to form links between her instinctual automatic actions and their outcomes, and in time these links will result in voluntary control over her behaviour. So, initially, she automatically turns her head to any sound – as the family dog comes into the room, say – but she will progressively anticipate and mentally represent the special sound of the dog and search him out voluntarily, rather than simply turn to the barking sound as a reflex. To acquire a sense of self is by no means easy, however. First and foremost, it involves the distinction of the self from others. The baby needs to learn that although she must depend on those around her for her care and well-being, she nevertheless is an autonomous being who can act

This ten-month-old is clearly having great fun interacting with the face in the mirror, but at this age she probably doesn't know it is a reflection of her own face that she is so drawn to.

alone. The basic foundations of this knowledge of 'me' emerge during the second half of the first year of life. By roughly two years of age, the child's self-concept becomes increasingly complex, and the use of personal terms such as 'I', 'me' or 'mine' allows her to communicate her sense of self directly.

How can we investigate self-awareness in the baby? One means is to examine a baby's response to her mirror image. During the first three months, an infant shows little interest in her own reflection. It is something to look at, much like the poster on the wall or the television. Unlike mum's interesting face, it doesn't say anything, and it isn't warm and prickly like dad's. By four months, however, the baby becomes interested in what she sees in the mirror, and may reach out towards an object in the reflection. But at this stage, she has not yet made the distinction between the mirror image and the real thing, and will stare at the face in the mirror in much the same way as she will stare at your face. There seems to be no indication that the baby knows that she is looking at her own face. This can be tested by examining the baby's reaction to the mirror reflection of an object approaching from behind. At this age, the baby will not turn around to look for the object, but will expect the object to be in front of her.

Over the next four months, the baby becomes increasingly interested in what she sees in mirrors, and will often smile at her own reflection. This is not an early indication of vanity! It is doubtful that at this stage the baby is aware who it is that she sees in the mirror when she looks at herself: she may well think it's another smiling baby. The next stage towards self-recognition develops between ten and eleven months of age. The baby now recognises that what she is looking at is not real, but a reflection. She will turn around to look for a toy approaching her from behind, if she sees this in the mirror (*see feature, page 52*). This step may not yet be more than a development in her spatial representation of the immediate environment. She has formed a mental picture of

Does your baby know her own reflection?

There are many little experiments parents can try at home to follow their baby's developing self-awareness. Hold your four-month-old within arm's reach of a mirror and have your partner or friend approach a toy from behind, so your baby can clearly see it in the mirror reflection but not out of the corner of her eye. Encourage her to respond to what she is looking at with prompts such as: 'Where's the toy? Can you see the toy?' A common reaction will be for your baby to reach out to the reflection of the toy, paying little attention to her own face in the mirror. But after you get that response, try making a noise with the toy. Your baby will turn to look at it. Then hide the toy, attract the baby's attention back to the mirror and lower the toy once more silently. This hide-and-seek exercise can be lots of fun for everyone. Not only can you watch your baby's development, but you are actively taking part in it by encouraging her learning process.

During the next four months, watch your baby communicate with mirror images by smiling or gurgling at them. This can be very entertaining. Play peek-a-boo in the mirror, talk to your baby as she watches your reflection, or just let her study her own face quietly. When your baby reaches ten months, try the approaching toy test again. This time, you can expect her to turn around and look for the toy.

The red spot game can be played with your baby once she's a year old. Use something easily removable and not harmful to her delicate skin, such as blusher, and apply it carefully to her forehead or the end of her nose while she's sleeping. (A little sticker is unsuitable as she may detect its presence before looking in the mirror.) Make sure you leave some time between putting on the red spot and going to the mirror, so she makes no direct connection between the two acts. Does she point at the spot in the mirror or attempt to rub it off? What do you think her reaction indicates? Another variation of this game demonstrates your baby's memory for your face. Place a sticker on your nose while your baby is looking in the mirror – without her seeing you do this, of course. Then see if she turns around to examine your face when she sees your reflection with its new addition.

her environment and recognises that it is the same as the one in the mirror. So she uses this information to situate the approaching toy in relation to the rest of the things around her.

However, it is still unclear whether the baby has a clear picture or memory of her own face. The evidence suggests that this comes later. At ten months, if a red spot is surreptitiously painted on to the baby's forehead before she looks in the mirror, she will not attempt to rub it off when she sees her own reflection. It takes another six to eight months before the child makes the connection between what she is seeing (a red spot on the forehead of her reflection) and what is on her face at that moment. So, by eighteen months, we see a clear demonstration of self-awareness. For the next two years, the child will continue to show a lot of interest in her reflection, studying the way she looks, practising making faces, or talking to her reflection.

Although scientists still have to pinpoint the exact mechanisms involved in gaining a self-image, research with primates shows that day-to-day interaction with others plays an important role in this process. Chimpanzees are one of the only other species to display self-recognition of their mirror reflections.

Interestingly, however, young chimps who have been brought up in complete social isolation never display this ability. It seems that without constant feedback from others, from day one, developing a self-concept is particularly difficult. It is through studying other people in her environment and their reactions to her that the infant is ultimately able to learn about herself.

DISCOVERING GENDER Despite the fact that children do not develop a comprehensive gender concept until they are about three years old, babies start learning about some important sex-typing characteristics from the day they are born. Using the experimental sucking technique described on page 16, scientists have been able to show that as early as seven months, babies correctly discriminate between stereotyped photos of male and female faces. They have already formed a very basic sex category based on particular cues such as hairlines, facial features and facial hair. Interestingly, even at one month infants can correctly match a female voice with a female face, so long as both the voice and face are highly stereotyped, yet it is not until much later – around twelve months – that they can correctly match a male voice to a male face. The reason for this is probably because mothers are the primary carers during the first few weeks of life, giving baby the chance to learn about female characteristics such as face shape and voice pitch early on, and to form important links between them. To match a voice to a face, the baby needs to be able to make difficult connections between what she hears and sees, and it is only after repeated exposure and the opportunity to compare male and female voices and facial features that the baby can piece together her knowledge about these differences between the sexes.

Although babies are actively learning about gender during their first eighteen months, it is very difficult to ascertain precisely how much they know until the latter half of the second year when pronounced sex-typed behaviour becomes apparent in general interaction and in play. To look ahead briefly, your child will probably use the labels 'girl' and 'boy' correctly with respect both to herself and to others (adults, siblings, peers) some time between the ages of two and three, though it isn't until around her third birthday that she will be able correctly to communicate the

Just after I was born, all the visitors who came to see us kept asking the same question: 'Is it a boy or a girl?' I thought I was just a baby. I didn't realise there was any difference between me and my brother. How will I know how to be a 'girl'?

The sex you are born affects everything about you – your temperament, your behaviour, even the way others behave towards you. In fact, your gender will play a part in shaping the whole course of your life. This may sound heavy, but don't worry, you won't have to take classes in how to become a girl – it'll happen automatically. You'll learn about your own gender, and the differences between you and your brother, over the next two or three years.

idea of gender permanence and consistency – that is, will be confident about correctly answering questions such as: 'Have you ever been a boy?' 'Were you a boy when you were born?' or 'When you are grown up, will you be a mummy or a daddy?' Around this age, too, parents may begin to notice increased sex-stereotyping in their child's general behaviour, play activities, choice of toys and even choice of friends. Although there are exceptions, many little boys will engage in more physical play such as rough-and-tumble, refuse to take on certain roles such as the nurse in a doctors-and-nurses game, and choose lorries instead of dolls to play with. In contrast, many three-year-old

ADULT PRECONCEPTIONS ABOUT INFANT BEHAVIOUR

There is a wealth of research documenting gender-related attitudes and behaviour of parents towards their babies and young children. In one experiment, expectant parents were told the sex of several babies of nine months to three years and asked to rate the infants using sex-typed characteristics, such as 'strong' versus 'weak' or 'active' versus 'inactive'. Results showed that the adults rated each infant according to the label (boy or girl) that the child had been given, regardless of the baby's actual characteristics. Other data have indicated that parents are more likely to describe newborn girls as 'smaller', 'softer', more 'fragile' and as having 'finer features' than newborn boys, irrespective of whether this is really true. Further research has demonstrated that if you show a group of adults a video recording of a baby dressed in blue, moving around in a cot, they will interpret the baby's movements as being typical of a strong baby boy. But if the same baby's clothes are changed to pink using a simple video editing technique, the same adults will interpret the movements as typical of dainty girls!

Studies comparing the ways mothers and fathers interact and play with boy and girl toddlers (by videotaping adult–infant pairs playing together) found that, however unintentionally, parents often encouraged certain sex-typed activities. Thus, fathers would initiate rougher play with boys, but engage in quiet, non-intrusive play with girls. Although their approach was often more subtle, mothers also rewarded appropriate gender-related behaviour. For example, they would show marked enthusiasm when a baby girl chose nurturing games such as fantasy play with dolls, or when baby boys engaged in construction-type play with blocks. Both parents would also steer the child towards playing with certain toys as opposed to others, according to their sex. A general finding from such research is that parental attitudes, behaviours and expectations become increasingly gender specific as the child grows and develops.

Research has shown that adults – and fathers in particular – tend to handle boys more roughly and throw them around more playfully than girls.

girls will select sedentary and constructive play such as tea parties, constructions and puzzles, and will be more inclined to ask what role or game the other child would like to play.

Despite parents' attempts to have girls play with lorries and boys with dolls, each sex has *already* learned to categorise gender. What's more, the majority of these learned distinctions are unwittingly and subtly given by parents. Even a very young baby will begin to note the differences between the way the sexes behave in everyday life, and the way they react to her (*see opposite*). The child's primary sources of sex-typed information are therefore her parents. Indeed, unbeknownst to her (and often to them), parents frequently form a gender-specific idea of their child even *before* her birth! Parents-to-be often speculate about the sex of their unborn baby: 'He kicks so vigorously, he must be a footballer!' Then, the suspense of labour reaches its peak with the question 'Is it a boy or a girl?' From the first moments of life, the baby's sex will determine to a very significant extent how her parents hold her, interpret her behaviour and how they respond to her. It also has subtle effects on their expectations and values regarding the future life of their baby, in spite of parents' conscious aims to resist gender stereotyping. It is through the feedback the baby gets from those around her that she forges her own identity.

How do I become part of my family?

How come you both cried when I was born? And why is it that even though I keep you awake all night with constant feeding and nappy changing, you still seem to love me? I find I want to be with you more than anything. Where do all these feelings come from?

The emotions that have awakened in you and your parents are the main ingredients of what is called 'bonding'. The relationships you form now are very important in shaping the way you'll respond to other people throughout your life. You'll learn how to trust people and how to form strong and secure attachments with others. Right from birth, every experience you share with your parents contributes to the closeness that grows between you.

BONDING The roots of the bonding process start to grow during the last three months of pregnancy. This is when the baby's movements become increasingly noticeable, and parents often begin to communicate regularly with their foetus. Talking to the expectant mother's growing bump, playing little games by making the baby respond with kicks to a finger placed on the belly, or setting aside special moments to relax together – these all help parents-to-be feel close to their unborn baby. This relationship is consolidated at birth, the moment you and your baby cuddle and look into each other's eyes for the first time, and is strengthened by every experience you share together – the first feed, the first bath, even the first nappy! But it doesn't stop there: bonding will continue throughout your lives.

The complete dependence of a tiny baby sets the agenda for the parent–child relationship. Newborns demonstrate selective attention to human faces and voices, and learn to recognise their parents within days.

The infant's face brightens as she sees her parents approach. This immediately elicits love in her parents and is interpreted by them as proof that they are special to their baby, which in turn strengthens the two-way relationship. Infants also display certain reflexive behaviours which, although not intentional, seem like an amazing design of Nature specifically to promote bonding. For example, only moments after birth, newborns respond to their parents' sticking their tongues out or making mouth movements by doing the same thing, as though these 'imitations' were part of a dialogue (*see pages 85–6*). And parents react with expressions of joy when they think their newborn is responding to them

Bonding is a vital part of your new baby's development. The establishment of a secure and fulfilling relationship with the primary care-giver (usually the mother at first), paves the way for the child's future relationships, be it with other members of the family, friends, and eventually, lifelong partners. It is thought that the attachment between mother and baby, if close and secure, establishes in the child a basic trust in other people. Through the first attachments a child establishes with her parents, she is able to form an internal model of how the social world functions which, in turn, enables her to situate herself within her environment. Such a model is based on a series of interaction experiences, accumulated from the very start of life. This gradual process takes some years, but

Babies are born with certain characteristics that generate caring feelings in the people around them. Their plump cheeks, big eyes with large pupils, soft skin and clumsy movements make us want to nurture them.

Getting to know your baby

From the very first day of your baby's life, talking to her and maintaining frequent physical contact are good ways of developing a strong bond between you. But don't be hard on yourself if the feelings you expect do not awaken instantly. Get close to your baby gradually by making eye contact, learning about and responding to her behaviour when you are feeding, changing or playing with her, and use every opportunity to communicate with her. If you feel lost, seek help and advice. You mustn't punish yourself by keeping things bottled up. Don't forget that after birth, a woman's hormone levels are still fluctuating and she is usually exhausted physically. This can have a direct bearing on how she adjusts to the change from being pregnant to caring for her new baby. Many mothers experience feelings of loss about not being pregnant anymore. Others worry about the frailty of their newborns, and feel clumsy and awkward about handling them. These are all normal reactions. Share your feelings with your partner, friends or other new mothers — you will discover that you are not alone in feeling a bit lost.

Fathers can sometimes feel a little left out at first, and worry that their new baby will not bond with them as easily as with mum, especially if she is breast-feeding and he is out at work all day. There are many things couples can do to promote bonding with both parents. Set aside some special time each day for dad and baby to spend alone together. Share care-giving activities as much as possible to ensure that your baby learns that both parents can provide her with what she needs. Also, try setting the alarm a little earlier than necessary so that the three of you can have a daily cuddle in bed before work.

Even if mum is breast-feeding, dad can share in the closeness of feeding by giving his baby a regular bottle feed using expressed milk. Mum will appreciate the help!

early relationships are utterly crucial. Insecure attachments in early life can have serious long-term consequences, reflected in a failure to thrive both physically and emotionally.

The aim of the baby's first attachment behaviours is to obtain warmth, comfort and security. Very young babies communicate their attachment to their parents through crying, smiling, eye contact and vocalising. In exchange, the parents encourage this communication with words, cuddles, by imitating baby's facial expressions or sounds and through constant care-giving. Parental body language and tone of voice also play an important role.

As the baby grows, she gradually learns how to predict her parents' behaviour. She manages to work out what makes them smile and what encourages them to pay even more attention to her, information she can then use to promote further mutually satisfying exchanges. The onset of the social smile, at around two months old, is a perfect example of this. 'Smiling' before this age occurs simply in response to physical sensations such as an air bubble in the stomach, being stroked on the cheek or contorting the facial muscles. From the baby's point of view it is not really a smile, but its resemblance to smiling drives the parent to react to the infant with enthusiasm. So later, once the baby learns to control her smile, she can begin to associate smiling with the joy it clearly brings to her parents and others. You will now notice your baby smiling away like a Cheshire cat at every opportunity (*see also pages 87–90*). Later still, this repertoire will be extended as the toddler discovers ways of making people laugh. Thus, by smiling or uttering 'ma' or 'da', the child provides her parents with rewarding behaviours and ensures that the relationship is pleasurable for all concerned.

A few months after birth, the baby becomes even more aware of the emotional flow between herself and her parents. She will now begin to act in ways that are specifically designed to encourage loving responses from her mother and father. For example, as you approach the cot, your baby may stretch out her arms towards your face, indicating her wish to be picked up and cuddled. And when you hold her, she may now intentionally snuggle her face against your neck, embrace you with her little arms or stroke your face. Although you have been experiencing similar close contact with your baby since she was born, you will now find that she has become a far more active participant. This is because she is gradually gaining knowledge about the reciprocal emotions that exist within social relationships.

As a baby becomes mobile, the world takes on a whole new meaning. She now has the ability not only to move away from mum or dad, in order to explore her surroundings, but also to seek proximity to them if she feels the need for security. Proximity-seeking is a sign of a healthy, secure bond and this behaviour should not be interpreted as shyness *per se*. In fact,  it is the most securely attached babies who, though regularly seeking contact or closeness with their parents in a new situation, will at the same time show greatest confidence in exploring new things and situations. If baby finds herself in an unfamiliar room with mum or dad, for example, she will set herself an area within a safe distance from the parent from which she can explore happily. The parent acts as a secure base for the investigative child. She will often seek eye or physical contact, or just check at intervals that her parent is still there, in order to reassure herself that it is safe to continue her activities.

I'm ten days old and my favourite pastime is looking at faces. I've already got to know mum and dad's faces really well. But today I got very confused. The person who picked me up had mum's voice and smell, but didn't look like mum. Why couldn't I recognise her?

What confused you was that your mum had a haircut that made her look different. At this age, your vision is not yet completely developed, so you can't see the details of her face very clearly. Over the past few days you've learned to recognise her from the outline of her face and head. The shape of her hair is a particularly useful marker for you, so when she changed her hairstyle, you were no longer able to recognise her. In about two months, you won't have that problem, as you'll know her face by its internal features.

THE ABILITY TO RECOGNISE FACES Psychologists have long debated the issue of infant face recognition. Babies seem to arrive into the world with a preference for looking at faces or face-like objects. Only moments after birth, they already appear mesmerised by the faces that approach and communicate with them. Some scientists have therefore suggested that humans are born programmed to attend to face-like patterns. This serves a vital function in helping to shape the infant's first experiences, as it ensures that she learns quickly about humans, especially her mother whose face she watches intently as she takes her first meals.

During the first few weeks of life, a baby can focus only up to about 25 cm (10 inches) – almost exactly the distance between a baby's eyes and her mother's face when she is breast-feeding. The newborn processes objects mainly by their outline rather than their internal features, so she will initially get to know her mother's 'face' by her hairline and the general shape of her head, rather than her specific facial characteristics. Parent–baby communication during feeds is extremely important, as this is a time when the baby's visual senses are stimulated. The brain uses this stimulation to form important neural links that enable the baby to create a mental image of the special outline of her parent's face.

Researchers have devised some fascinating experiments on newborn vision and face processing. Studies of early vision demonstrate that the newborn scans her environment for things that provide her developing visual

Even during the early weeks of life, babies will respond more positively to the appearance of their parents' faces than to any other face.

system and brain with the maximum amount of stimulation. She actively searches for, and is attracted to, objects that move and change, and that have a high degree of contrast, interesting contours and complex patterns (*see pages 162–5*). Infants also show a clear preference for symmetrical designs, as well as circular rather than squared outlines. These qualities all apply to the human face. What makes the face particularly attractive is the fact that it not only provides the baby with the sort of visual stimulation she is actively seeking, but that it also speaks and makes eye contact. So the human face, or more specifically, the faces of mother and father, provide the infant with the richest form of stimulation available during her first few weeks of life. Paying particular attention to parents' faces serves the added purpose of promoting interaction with the primary care-givers, which is crucial for the baby's physical and social development.

The results of experiments on newborn face recognition show that at first infants like to look at any face-like stimulus. This might be a photo of a real face, or a drawing of an oval outline containing three blobs for the two eyes and mouth (see boxed feature, *page 16*). They also show a preference for looking at the outlines of their mothers' or fathers' faces over those of strangers. By two months of age, the baby's visual system is developed enough to begin processing the *internal* details of the human face – the shape and colour of the eyes, the mouth, the nose, the chin, dad's stubble! The baby now begins to form clearer memories of individual faces, and will recognise her parents even if they are wearing glasses, hats, or have new haircuts. Your baby will know your face so well that she will be able to discriminate between a photo of your face and that of a stranger.

By the time they are eight weeks old, babies no longer show interest in the abstract face-like pattern with the three blobs. They prefer to study real faces or complete drawings of faces, paying attention to all the different internal features that make each face unique. By five months, they even start to find static faces boring and show a significant preference for active faces with changing expressions. They will now lose interest in a person's face if it doesn't react, change, communicate or respond to interaction. In fact, if you put on a still face in front of a young baby for a certain length of time, and resist the temptation to respond to the baby's efforts to communicate with you, the baby may soon become bored with looking at your face and look elsewhere for something more interesting. She may even show considerable distress and start crying. It may take some time to calm her down, even after you resume normal interaction.

Quite early on, babies also begin to take notice of other important facial features that give them a clue to the person's age, sex, and ethnicity. Curiously, infants can be smarter than adults in this respect. Until the baby's brain becomes specialised in recognising the faces of those most familiar to her, she is actually able to differentiate between endless numbers of faces from other races and even other species – unlike adults, a young baby can discriminate between different chimpanzee faces. This is not something she will be able to do for very long, however. As it matures, the human brain actively selects what is most relevant to daily life. So by ten months, the baby's capacity for face discrimination of all ethnicities and other species is considerably reduced as she becomes progressively expert in the kinds of face that are significant in her own environment. As we shall see on page 94, infants also find it more difficult to distinguish between the sounds of different languages as they grow older, probably for similar reasons.

Without even realising it, I've been able to learn to tell the difference between mum and dad. It's uncanny, but I can tell straight away which of them is approaching, holding me, or changing my nappy. How do I tell them apart so well?

Even in the womb, you began to recognise special things about your mum, such as the sound of her voice. Then, from the minute you were born, you started to become familiar with the way each of your parents looks, smells and moves. You've also picked up on subtle differences in the way they hold you, talk to you and react to you. Coming to know what's unique about each of your parents happens spontaneously as you form mental images of the world around you.

DISTINGUISHING BETWEEN PARENTS The newborn's sense of hearing is well developed, and she begins to process changes in vocal pitch and intonation as soon as she is born. However, before she is able to recognise, and therefore show a preference for, a particular individual's voice, the newborn must have been exposed to it long enough to form a memory of its distin-

Dad's low voice, his facial characteristics, the feel of his stubbly skin, the particular way he interacts – these all help baby differentiate between mum and dad.

guishing characteristics. At birth, she has already had plenty of exposure to her mother's voice from within. She has also heard her father's voice when her parents spoke to each other, but it was never very clear. So it may take a little while before she is able to distinguish between her father's voice and other male voices. Similarly, as a result of the early, close and frequent contact between mother and infant during her first few weeks in the outside world, the newborn very quickly learns to recognise her mother's face. However, if the father takes an active role in the care of his newborn, she soon gets to know the shape of his head and hairline, his eyebrows, beard or moustache, and to show a preference for his face too.

Research has demonstrated that early on infants also begin to learn about the way people move. They pay attention to the differences between the biological movement of living things and the artificial or mechanical motion of objects (*see also pages 179–80*). Scientists have studied this by showing infants two sets of light patterns on TV monitors and comparing the babies' responses. In one test, the light patterns were generated by attaching lights to the ankles, knees and hips of a moving person, and represented biological movement. All the baby saw on the screen were the patterns of moving lights on a dark background. In the other test, the light movements were generated by computer and represented artificial or abstract movement. Babies were given dummies attached to a computer and their sucking rates were recorded. The results indicated that babies as young as three months sucked harder and thereby showed a distinct preference for human biological movement over the artificial movement of objects. Making such early distinctions helps babies learn about the characteristics that differentiate an individual's gait. They can also start to note the general differences between male and female movements and mannerisms. This plays a vital role in helping infants form detailed memories of the defining characteristics of each parent.

During the first weeks of life, babies also become increasingly sensitive to the differences in the way each parent handles them – the different feel of dad's hug, mum's caress, and the special way each parent responds when she smiles, coos or kicks her legs. By three months, the baby has formed a very detailed memory of her parents. This then plays an increasingly influential role in the way she herself interacts with each of them and they, in turn, react to her. Parents may grow increasingly aware of distinct responses which their voices, smiles or cuddles get from their baby. For instance, seeing her mother approach may calm baby down in some circumstances, while hearing her father's voice nearby may cause her to become excited and kick her legs vigorously. A little later, she may hold out her arms to dad, who always gives in and picks her up.

SIBLING INTERACTION At first, the young baby seems only to have eyes for her parents. She does perceive the little face that peers into the cot every so often, but as it is not associated with being fed, cuddled or cared for, it holds as yet little meaning for her. By two or three months, the baby will recognise her brother's face, as she does other faces she sees regularly, but she will not yet actively seek his attention. Her mind is still firmly on mum and dad. By this stage, however, her growing attention to the visual environment means that she is becoming increasingly attentive to interesting toys, mobiles or anything colourful dangled in front of her. For the toddler who shows his little sister his prize possessions, it can now become more satisfying to get a response as she stares intently at his toy. By seven months of age, the baby is able successfully to match faces to voices, and she will begin to look in the direction of her brother if she hears him chatting nearby. Later, she will begin to form an even stronger attachment to her older siblings. Fascinated by the skill with which they can move and play, she is likely to spend hours lovingly watching them carry out their activities – despite the disdain (or even the odd jealous blow) she may receive in return.

Relationships with siblings are extremely important. During childhood, siblings often spend as much time with each other as they do with their parents, so the interaction between children has a significant impact on their later development. It contributes to the acquisition of language, play, the development of attachment and a general understanding of the world. However, infant responses to

Babies are often besotted with their older siblings: this eleven-month-old is taking a lesson in self-feeding from his big sister.

There's this little person who's always hanging around us. I've seen you cuddle him just like you cuddle me. He's even given me a few kisses, but they're usually followed by a nasty pinch! Who is this intruder, and why is his behaviour towards me so unpredictable?

He's not really an intruder, but he probably thinks you are! The little person who shares your parents with you is your older brother. Until now he's had mum and dad all to himself so it can be quite hard for him to adjust to having suddenly to share them with you. But once you're a little bigger it'll be more fun for both of you. He'll start to play with you and show you how to use his toys.

Overcoming sibling rivalry

A toddler often develops a love–hate ambivalence towards a new baby. If you are experiencing difficulties in getting your toddler used to his new sibling, there are several things you can try. It's always important to involve the older child from day one – that is, the day your pregnancy starts to show, rather than the day you bring baby home. Even if your child is not yet speaking, show him and talk to him about your growing tummy. Point out babies when you pass them in the street, and explain that mummy is carrying one inside her. Involve him in the preparations at home before the birth; let him investigate the nursery equipment, for example.

This is a time when you and everyone around needs to be especially encouraging and supportive of the older sibling. His self-esteem will be shaken by the arrival of a baby, and he needs to feel confident that he is still loved by those around him. Make a point of being particularly interested in his activities. Both parents should apportion special time each day to spend alone with the child, away from the new baby. The child's routines should carry on as normally as possible. Cutting out the bedtime story may not seem important to you when baby is screaming her head off in the next room, but to your older child it could be very upsetting. Organise treats or trips out to make him feel special. And whenever possible, involve him in activities surrounding the baby or around the house in general (although do keep a watchful eye out: even a well-intentioned toddler can be a bit rough with a baby, let alone a jealous one!). If he feels he is helping you in ways that the baby cannot, his self-confidence will be boosted.

their brothers or sisters have unfortunately been little studied – research into sibling relationships has concentrated on older children's reactions to the arrival of a new baby.

Young children react in different ways to the disruption created by a new arrival. Some will show great interest in mum's growing bump, and will seem excited when the baby is born. Invariably, however, a toddler's initial interest will turn to anxiety when he realises that his position in the family must be reestablished. Not being the baby anymore is one of the hardest things to come to terms with. A common reaction to this is regression. The toddler will revert to babyish behaviour: perhaps wetting the bed again, refusing to feed himself, wanting a bottle and generally seeking help or assistance with day-to-day activities that only weeks before he was so proud to manage alone. But don't despair if your child's previous development seems to take an about-turn with the arrival of the new baby: it's perfectly normal and is not a permanent setback. Be very patient and teach him again the things you taught him before. The child's self-confidence has been undermined by the changes that have taken place, and becoming dependent again is the only way he can be assured of competing for his parents' attention. This phase, during which the older child is rebuilding his identity and place within the family, can be very difficult for parents. They have to juggle between reassuring the child, and struggling with the physical and emotional demands of the newborn. But a few careful steps can soon resolve the upheavals in the home (see boxed feature opposite).

STRANGER AWARENESS When infants are very young, they will readily snuggle up in anyone's arms and let anyone attend to them. The baby at this stage is not aware of the complexities of her environment beyond her basic needs. She is in a state of ignorant bliss. It is only as she begins to perceive her world as a complicated and constantly changing place, and as her bonds with her parents grow deeper, that she develops certain anxieties. Although babies seem to exhibit a whole range of emotions from birth, these are largely physiologically driven: the baby cries not because she is 'sad' but because she is hungry; she looks content not because she is 'happy' but because she is full or her nappy has just been changed!

Around six months of age, the baby begins to show inhibition and wariness towards unfamiliar people, outside the immediate family. This coincides with the developmental stage when babies are able to form clear memories for individual faces, and compare new people with the internal template they have of their parents' faces. If the stranger's face doesn't match this, there is reason for the baby to feel apprehensive. This is *not* an indication of a shy temperament towards other people, it is simply that the baby has not yet built up a comprehensive enough repertoire of reactions to new happenings. Furthermore, while she has spent the last six months learning about mum and dad's behaviour, she is not yet sure what to expect from new people. Strangers have to become a little more familiar if they are not to be feared. So, during this phase it is important not to force new people and situations on to your baby. She needs to find balance within herself and discover in her own time how to deal with her anxieties. Gentle encouragement, comfort and plenty of patience are the best remedies. This stage of stranger anxiety is fairly short-lived, lasting a few months at most, and tends to be followed by a fear of separation from mum and dad (*see overleaf*).

I used to like being handed around from person to person. I found it interesting looking at different faces and I loved all the attention. But not any more. If someone approaches me now, I burst into tears and clutch mummy's leg. Is this just a phase I'm going through?

Yes, you do feel a bit shy right now, but this is a normal part of learning how to react to new people, outside your family. Until now, you were not aware of just how complicated the world is and concentrated on getting to know your mum and dad. But as your relationships with other people and your knowledge about your environment develop, so do certain anxieties. Rest assured though: this fear will soon pass.

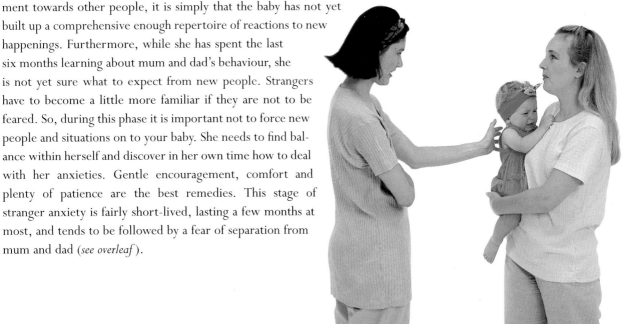

Even the most gregarious babies can go through a stage of fear of strangers, like this nine-month-old girl, clinging resolutely to her mum.

Recently, I've started getting anxious whenever you leave my side. I'm scared you won't come back. I don't want to play and I'm only happy again when you return. How do I know you won't leave me for good?

What you're experiencing now is 'separation anxiety'. It's an automatic reaction to being without mum or dad: you've become so used to depending on them, it's difficult for you to understand that they can't be with you all the time. You haven't yet realised that if they leave the room, it doesn't mean they've gone forever. Actually, your feelings are a sign that you have a strong bond with your parents. So don't worry; your fears will soon disappear.

SEPARATION ANXIETY From about one year onwards, young children often display anxious behaviour – crying, screaming, shouting, kicking – when they see their parent leaving the room. This is a response to what the child feels when her secure attachment with the parent is placed under threat by separation. The infant's protest has specific aims. It ensures that mother or father will return to comfort the baby; and it serves to reduce the likelihood that the parent will leave again. In some ways, then, the child is actively trying to restore the equilibrium by 'punishing' the care-giver for leaving her alone.

Since the infant cannot yet use words to communicate her feelings, the only coping strategy available to her is protest. Typically, she will become agitated and then upset upon seeing her mother or father leave the room. She may not consent to being consoled by another adult, but will remain distraught or distracted until the parent returns. Although parents should reassure their baby that they are coming back, there's obviously no point in stressing you'll only be away ten minutes because the baby has no concept of time; she may think she's being abandoned forever. Upon seeing mum or dad again, the child shows great enthusiasm or clinginess; she may continue crying for a little while in order to be held close, but will then return to playing happily within a safe distance from the parent. This behaviour is found in most young children who have developed a secure bond or attachment to their parents. In fact, psychologists have found that a child's display of separation anxiety is a reliable measure of the quality of her attachments. As such, it can be used as a predictive tool for later development, as early attachments are the prototype of later relationships. But other influences may also play a role in how children react in new situations. These render interpretations of infant behaviour a little less straightforward. For example, some scientists have pointed out that the child's individual temperament may have an important influence on how she responds to situations, as well as how parents react in return. Furthermore, early experiences can have a direct bearing on how a baby interprets being left alone, even for a brief moment. For instance, if a young infant is used to being regularly cared for by several different people from a very young age (grandparents, siblings, child minders, friends), she may not display as strong a reaction to separation as a baby who is cared for primarily by one parent.

How do I get to know other people?

UNDERSTANDING OTHERS HAVE INTEN-TIONS Imagine you are talking to a friend and she suddenly rushes out of the door closing it behind her. What is your reaction? You don't simply register the fact that she has left the room and that the door is shut. Nor do you merely think that she intended to leave the room and has fulfilled her goal. Instead, you generate a host of hypotheses about why she left the room: did she suddenly feel ill, had she forgotten to fill the meter for parking her car, had she heard her baby cry? Rather than just recording physical events, or treating your friend as an intentional being, you attribute mental thoughts to her and view her actions as a function of her thoughts. In other words, you have what is called a 'theory of mind' and interpret people's behaviour in terms of their intentions and what they think, rather than just what they do.

I've found that I am getting better and better at predicting what mum is about to do. I just have to watch her, and I seem to know that she is about to pick me up, or move the chair or go out of the room. Am I 'psychic'?

No, you don't have special powers to see into the future, you have simply become more aware of the relationship between different behaviours. By spending so much of your time gazing at your parents and following their every move, you are able to make connections between actions and their outcomes. And you are starting to understand that people have intentions that make them behave in specific ways.

Research on the development of a theory of mind in children shows that it progresses through two stages. The initial stage covers roughly the first six months of life. It involves coming to see others as 'intentional agents'. In other words, understanding other people's behaviour in terms of goals and the activities they carry out in order to achieve these goals. This understanding is a fundamental aspect of human intelligence.

One of the first ways an infant experiences intentionality is by following her parent's gaze. In doing so, she learns that looking at something and picking it up are two actions that are purposefully linked. So next time she sees her mother looking at the toy on the table, she will predict that mum intends to pick it up. This gaze-following takes up much of the baby's time during the first six months. It starts off relatively clumsily, with the infant only jerkily following her mother's gaze and ending up looking in the same general area, but not necessarily at the specific toy. Later the baby zeroes in on the precise object of attention.

Next the baby discovers that she herself is able to direct her mother's attention to an object by looking intently at it, then back at mum several times when she is paying attention to her. If she is right about the link between looking and picking up, she can now predict that her mother will pick up the object for her and hand it over. This process is called 'joint attention'. The important

WHAT DRIVES A BABY'S FEELINGS?

Everything we think, feel and do depends on the transmission of messages from one nerve cell or neuron to another. At birth, the network of connections between these neurons is rudimentary, but as the infant's neural circuits become progressively specialised, a group of cells deep in the centre of the brain becomes dedicated to the processing of emotions and social information. These pathways reside in what is known as the limbic system, which involves connections between structures in the outer layer or cortex of the brain, particularly the part known as the orbital frontal cortex, and structures deep within the brain or subcortex, especially the amygdala. Electrical impulses carry messages from one neuron to another by activating structures a little like trapdoors, through which substances called chemical neurotransmitters are released into the microscopic gap or synapse between the neurons. These neurotransmitters cross from one neuron to a number of others, transmitting messages (or brain waves) across the brain at a speed quicker than one hundredth of a second.

The cells in the limbic system release more than fifty different types of chemical neurotransmitters. Some of these make the infant feel happy and send messages to the muscles to relax, for instance when an infant processes her mother's smiling face or gentle voice, while others are released when the infant is angry or scared, making her muscles become tense. These reactions are automatic and continue throughout life. They enable us rapidly to assess whether a situation is safe or dangerous.

The amygdala is crucial for learning to react appropriately to dangerous events. It also plays an important role in understanding how others feel when they appear scared or distressed, in other words in the ability to empathise. Brain imaging studies show the amygdala to be particularly active in response to fearful, sad or happy facial expressions, while the orbital front cortex becomes increasingly active as levels of anger increase.

Some researchers argue that there are two parallel pathways for processing emotional stimuli. One pathway operates between structures *within* the subcortex (such as the thalamus and the amygdala) and gives rise to rapid and relatively crude emotional responses such as rage and aggression. More refined responses, which enable the infant to assess contextual and subtle emotional cues – for instance, the inconsistency the baby detects if she hears a happy voice but sees an angry face – require connections between areas in the cortex (the prefrontal cortex) and the subcortex (the hippocampus); these develop only later in infancy. Connections also exist to a much older part of the brain, the olfactory lobe, which may explain why scents like that of milk, perfume or a particular room are so evocative of mood and feeling in both children and adults. The pathways that develop between subcortical and cortical areas are crucial for socio-emotional development. Indeed, studies of infant monkeys have shown that damage to the limbic frontal lobes gives rise to an inability to display appropriate responses to social events in everyday life.

point here is that underlying the skill of joint attention is a basic understanding that people's behaviour is driven by specific intentions. So, human activity can then be interpreted by the child in terms of specific outcomes. By twelve months, babies are already quite good at this, although they have not yet realised that intentions do not always match the situations or the behaviour of people. They have no understanding that people can hold wrong beliefs, tell lies, or deceive one another (*see also page 75*).

The second stage in the process of developing a theory of mind is more complicated than the first, and takes another three years to become established. This involves seeing people in a very new light. People are no longer simply intentional agents, but mental agents. In other words, it is not enough to be able to predict their behaviour on the basis of their goals: the child is now aware of a need to understand something about a person's thoughts and beliefs before that person's actions can be predicted. The ability to understand how others think, and eventually to learn how to predict and influence what they are thinking, comes much later than understanding intentionality and requires several years of experience of the world.

I keep acting like a clown lately, doing foolish things on purpose and pulling silly faces just to make people laugh. Why do I find this so much fun?

Not only do you feel you are making someone happy by your actions, but their laughter makes you laugh too! During the past nine months, you've discovered a lot about why people do things or react in certain ways, and you're now in a position to use what you've learned to entertain those around you. Because you remember how a game of peek-a-boo makes you laugh, you play the same game with mum to amuse her.

TEASING AND HUMOUR From the age of about three months, babies begin to recognise the difference between an angry and a pleased tone of voice, and over the next few months they will learn which of their actions will elicit which response. Parents' early interaction with their infant centres very much on encouraging her to be alert, to notice and react to things, and later to smile and chuckle. For the parent, these reactions are visible proof that they are stimulating their baby in a positive way. Parents then reinforce these responses in their child by giving them additional encouragement.

By around eight or nine months old, your baby's memory has developed significantly (*see pages 156–61*). She is able to remember a whole repertoire of behaviours that will result in the kind of attention she likes best – extra cuddles, praise, smiles and laughter. She may even attempt to mimic the little games you play with her – teasing by holding out a toy and snatching it away just as you are about to take it; or playing her own version of peek-a-boo. Teasing games also form part of learning about giving and sharing. Although these games can begin as early as six months old, it will be some time before your baby will actually happily give you her toy so you can play with it yourself: teasing you does not entail having to give up her possessions. In fact, the toy is largely incidental in this act. Neither is she trying to fool you by making you believe you will get the toy and then withdrawing it from your reach. At this early stage, teasing games are simply imitations of behaviour the baby knows will result in laughter.

Mum keeps talking to me about something called play group. She says I'm going to meet lots of other kids. I'm feeling a bit worried though. Will I know how to make friends?

No, at first you won't automatically know how to make friends. Up to now your social network hasn't stretched much beyond mum and dad. But there's a whole world of interesting people out there – other adults, other children – and gradually you'll learn how to approach them, play with them, become friends and enjoy your social life.

MAKING FRIENDS Very young babies tend to have eyes only for their parents, and it takes some months before they show much more than a passing interest in others. But as the first year wears on, the baby's developing relationships with her parents, siblings and other relatives give her the opportunity to learn a number of vital social and motor skills. As her social world expands and she comes to understand the rules and conventions governing much of her parents' behaviour, she slowly learns to apply these skills to new situations such as interacting with other babies and children. Her improved motor coordination allows her to hold out toys in an invitation to play, point towards interesting things, 'speak' to her new playmates using various sounds or her own form of language and even, a little later, toddle towards potential friends.

Making friends is a tricky process, however, that doesn't always go smoothly. At first, babies lack the skills of subtlety and social niceties, and may often appear quite aggressive, abrupt or even mean to one another for no apparent reason (*see the photograph opposite*). Although your baby has been studying social rules for many months by watching your reactions to her own behaviour, as well as your reactions to other people, successfully applying these rules to others is not always easy. She may register a give-and-take inter-action, for example, but perhaps not realise that something has to be offered *before* it is taken!

You'll notice that when you put two babies down next to each other, they often show mutual interest in what the other is doing, but will not really play *together*. Known as 'parallel play', this form of indirect interaction often also involves imitation. The two babies will sit next to each other and their actions will become increasingly coordinated. However, their games will still not amalgamate into joint activity. Playing together is much more exacting as it involves sharing toys and sharing control over the progress of the game itself. The child also has to learn to accept that her playmates' wishes may differ from

Happily absorbed in their own games, these babies are engaged in 'parallel play': they aren't yet mature enough to truly join in a single game together.

Raising a sociable baby

Like older children and adults, some babies are better at making friends than others. But there are many ways in which parents can help the process along. Give your baby as many opportunities as possible to meet different kinds of people. Encourage interaction with other family members, family friends and visitors, even people you meet in the street or the shop. Your child will watch and learn from your own interaction with others. Always be there to reassure her when she is faced with a new person. Join a parent and baby group if there is one available in your area.

These provide your baby with the perfect opportunity to expand her social network in a safe and comforting environment. Small, informal groups are good preparation for nursery school, where your child will be faced with much larger groups of children and teachers in a more formal setting.

While she learns to play with her peers, you should respond to your child's activities with lots of encouragement. But unless she turns to you for help, don't interfere, even if you see her getting into difficulty. It is important for her to have the space to make mistakes and social blunders from which she can learn about the world of people.

her own, and to find ways to deal with this appropriately. This is all part of the difficult process of becoming a member of society. Early friendships are very much the product of individual encounters. They may span only the length of one game, and may need to be forged again at the next meeting. Indeed, it is often the baby with the best toy who will be chosen as the next candidate 'friend'! The infant's world is filled with so many new people and experiences right now that the value of a particular friendship cannot yet be put into perspective. A new encounter, even with a familiar person, still requires building up a different strategy of behaviour.

Faced with a room full of potential new friends, the toddler will try a number of different tactics in order to enter an established game. She may attempt a non-verbal approach, hovering on the outskirts of the group and either waiting for an indication that she has been accepted, or joining in gradually without upsetting the activities of her peers. Alternatively, she may opt for parallel play or mimicking, hoping her actions will become amalgamated into the ongoing game. The somewhat older child may try a more direct tactic, introducing her presence and willingness to play with words: 'Can I play too?' Unfortunately these approaches are not always successful, and rejection can be upsetting. Therefore, it is important for parents to be available to their infant when she is first faced with the new task of making friends. Gentle encouragement can go a long way.

LOOKING AHEAD **It's very easy for adults to interpret infant behaviour as manipulative (crying, say, 'just to be difficult'), but while young babies can assert their likes and dislikes to a certain extent, they are cognitively incapable of deliberately deceiving anyone. It isn't until they reach 18–24 months that they gain sufficient self-awareness to show signs of truly independent thought and behaviour. This stage of development can be difficult for parents: their hitherto easy-going baby becomes a stubborn little rascal, prone to temper tantrums and phoney tears. But tricky though this period can be, you may be comforted to know that these are actually positive signs that your child is acquiring a more mature under-standing of herself and others, which will allow her to sympathise and interact with her family and friends in more complex and varied ways.**

BECOMING ASSERTIVE Self-assertion has its roots in early infancy when babies gradually progress from reflex-driven behaviour to increasingly con-trolled, voluntary actions. These developments – which include controlling facial expressions, moving the arms and hands in order to reach or point, and producing increasingly complex vocalisations – lead to the specialisation of various areas of the brain and allow the baby increasingly to influence her environ-ment and the people in it. By around 24 months, the drive to gain fuller independence is felt strongly by the child and becomes worryingly apparent to her parents! Although this new drive is evidenced by dif-ficult and often tiresome behaviour, parents should interpret attempts to be assertive as a positive expression of their child's growing independence and abilities rather than as defiance and naughtiness.

One of the first symptoms of the strong impulse for independence is the toddler becoming a stickler for rules. Two-year-olds fixate on certain rules they have learned through observation. They gradually form concepts about the way things ought to be, and will get very upset and even angry if, for example, toys are put away in the wrong box or their favourite plastic duck is missing at bath-time. This period is often referred to as 'the terrible twos' because toddlers quite suddenly start throwing unexplainable tantrums. Having been so easy to please up to now, your baby may now grow increas-ingly demanding and bad-tempered. This is a time for adherence to all her routines, however petty and arbitrary they may seem to you. It's also a time

I now find myself saying, 'No! meedooit!' to mum every time she tries to help me. I want to do everything for myself, even though I often make a mess of things and get all worked up. Why am I being so naughty all of a sudden?

You're not being naughty. You're trying to establish some independence by attempting to do things your parents have always done for you. Pushing away offers of help is your way of asserting yourself and of better controlling what goes on around you. It doesn't always go as smoothly as you want, because you're still very restricted in what you can actually do on your own. But it's perfectly normal for you to experience frustra-tion and even rage as a result of your inabilities.

for lots of patience! Parents can take heart from the knowledge that this is a rather short-lived phase in their child's development. Surprisingly, however, the new drive for independence is often accompanied by an increase in the use of 'social referencing'. This is when toddlers check their parents' reactions to a new experience or stimulus before deciding how to respond to it themselves. So if father and child encounter a large dog while in the street, the toddler will often look up at her dad's face and gauge his response in order to know whether to be scared of the dog or whether to approach and stroke it. These behavioural developments seem to contradict each other, but by behaving in seemingly contradictory ways the toddler achieves a crucial balance between being daringly independent and cleverly cautious. The terrible twos are difficult for both child and parent, but form a necessary part of development and must be dealt with carefully if the child is to emerge strengthened in her independence, yet respectful of sensible rules.

Managing the terrible twos

Two-year-olds behaving badly are testing limits – the limits of your patience, the limits of the rules you set and also, importantly, the limits of their own ability to affect or change the world around them. In other words, your child is actively pushing situations to their utmost confines so as to discover what happens when things and situations are not as they should be. Often, the best way of dealing with the frustrating demands of the toddler is to purposely give in and let the child find out that her wishes are inappropriate for herself. So, for instance, if she insists on wearing her favourite woollen jumper on a hot summer's day, let her. She will soon find it uncomfortable and sweaty, and take it off of her own accord. Give her a chance to learn from her mistakes. This is the only way the rules she has learned and is inappropriately testing in this situation will be altered to suit a new context. Although leaving your child to make her own decisions is often advisable, there are obviously times when it is necessary to simply remove her from a dangerous situation by picking her up and physically

restraining her from making the wrong choice or a risky mistake. The best tactic then is to try to distract her from her immediate concern by turning her attention to something new and interesting.

Most toddlers over eighteen months have the occasional tantrum. If your child has a fit of temper, calm, firm words from you may help soothe his anger.

LYING AND DECEPTIVE BEHAVIOUR Imagine playing a game such as poker without realising that your opponent had concealed intentions or that you needed to hide your own! You would be incapable of using your wit to win the game. During our day-to-day lives, we constantly calculate, predict and manipulate one another's behaviour – when we play games, do business or just interact. Without tactics and knowledge about each other's thoughts and beliefs, this would be impossible. Amazingly, children begin to learn about these hidden dimensions of social life at an early age.

Even before the toddler has fully mastered language, she can display some signs of deceptive-like behaviour. For example, she may pretend to be hurt in order to get an extra cuddle. You shouldn't see this form of manipulation as lying, however, because your child is not concerned with what you actually think or believe. She is merely acting out a habitual scene to elicit the predicted, desired response. If, on the other hand, she were to hide your keys under the pillow when you turned your back, and then pretended she'd not seen them when you asked her, you could conclude that she was intentionally trying to make you hold a false belief. But this level of understanding about other people's beliefs isn't usually reached until around three or four years of age.

The child goes through several stages of 'lying' before being able really to deceive others successfully. Early examples are often quite amusing. For instance, a toddler may state very assertively: 'I didn't spill the juice, and I won't do it again.' This early form of cover-up is designed merely to avoid punishment, not to sow false thoughts in your mind. Young children also tell untruths in order to boost their self-image. They may brag to their little friends about fictitious toys they own or abilities they have. These crude forms of deception may seem harmless and even entertaining to adults. However, they should be discouraged. Parents should not reinforce this behaviour by responding to it with extra attention or amusement. Having said that, the development and use of deceptive behaviour can actually be seen as a positive sign, in that it shows that the child is gaining an increasingly sophisticated understanding of other people's minds. Without an insight into others' thoughts and intentions, we couldn't become writers, politicians or simply good parents.

My sister Lucy left her teddy bear on the chair, and while she was in the bath I saw my brother pick it up and hide it. But when she came back she looked for the teddy on the chair, even though it's now under the bed. Is she stupid?

No, her actions were quite normal under the circumstances, because she didn't know your brother was playing a trick on her. She didn't see the teddy bear being moved, so she thought it was still where she left it. You know, people's behaviour is influenced by what they think, and sometimes their thoughts don't match reality.

Your toddler's crocodile tears are not designed to be deliberately deceitful: it may simply be his way of asking for a hug before he has the words to express his emotional needs.

The Road to Language

Most parents and scientists used to think that language acquisition only started some time between twelve and eighteen months, when toddlers produced their very first words. Research has now shown how wrong this was: the process actually begins much earlier! A baby's hearing system is well formed by the final trimester of pregnancy and the foetus is exposed to many sounds in utero. He pays close attention to his mother's voice as it reaches him through the amniotic fluid, as well as to the intonation patterns of his native tongue. So by the time he is born, he is already tuned in to the rhythms of speech.

After birth, babies will spend much of their time listening carefully to their mothers' or care-givers' voices, absorbing all sorts of information about language even though they don't yet have the cerebral maturity or control over the vocal apparatus to speak themselves. Yet the drive to communicate is such that babies develop many different ways of communicating or 'talking' to us well before they can utter their first words. Crying, for instance, has different acoustic properties, and parents quickly learn to interpret one cry to mean hunger, another to mean pain or discomfort and yet another to say 'I'm bored and I want attention right now!'

Dialogue between you and your baby occurs long before he understands or produces language. While feeding or being changed, he will react to your voice by kicking his feet or cooing.

He will express negativity by crying or withdrawing and positivity by smiling and stretching towards you. Later, when he wants something, he will use pointing and grunting until he gets the coveted object. Even once he is producing recognisable words, he will accompany them with lots of body gestures to enhance his efforts to be understood. You will quickly learn to understand his communicative attempts and respond to them so that the dialogue between you becomes increasingly rich.

In acquiring language, babies have to learn both to understand and to produce words. These two facets of language start in early infancy, well before anything recognisable is uttered. Very early on cooing, laughing and other such sounds are a sign that your baby is trying out his articulatory system. Towards the middle of the first year,

he will start using a series of language-like noises known as 'babbling'. Infants are sometimes even smarter than their parents! They can hear and produce subtle auditory distinctions from all the languages of the world, a talent of which adults are no longer capable once they've specialised in their native tongue.

First words appear any time between twelve and twenty months, some babies relentlessly trying to get their mouths around sounds early and others waiting until they are ready. Then, some time between eighteen and thirty months, you may witness a sudden increase in the rapidity with which your baby acquires new words. This is often known as the 'naming explosion'. However, language is multi-levelled. It is composed not only of words, but of meaningful parts of words and of sentences. So evidence for language acquisition is based on more than just producing a list of words. Children also have to learn about grammar. For example, we know that when the sound '-ed' is added to a verb it implies past tense (like walked, talked and raced), and when '-er' is added to a noun it means an agent who does a job (like baker, dancer and writer). Infants also need to learn about word order and other aspects of grammar.

Language also incorporates a level of what are called 'paralinguistic clues' like stress and intonation, which help us to determine whether we are being asked a question, ordered to do something, or are merely being told about an interesting fact. We pick up clues from faces as well, so if we cannot hear a voice because of background noise, we can lipread and look at the speaker's body language to guess at what the person is saying. We take all this for granted as we talk, but these complex and tightly related levels of language are things that your infant will have to learn over the first years of life. You will find yourself quite naturally helping your infant pay attention to all these different levels by using a special kind of language with him called 'motherese' – or, to be more correct now that fathers play an increasingly important role in child care, 'parentese'. This language, which parents use naturally, stresses different intonations in a sing-song manner that helps infants distinguish sounds, words and phrases. By the time your child is three or four years of age, he will be a pretty fluent speaker and by then you will find yourself naturally reducing the patterns of parentese and using increasingly adult-like language with him.

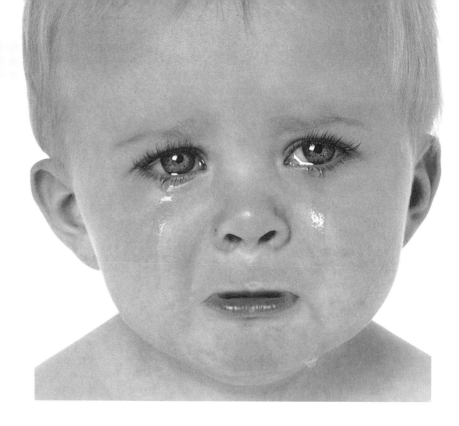

How do I communicate without words?

I've just made an interesting discovery. If I cry loud enough, mum comes and picks me up. Seems like a good way of getting her attention. But how come she seems to know exactly what I want each time I cry, even though I can't tell her?

Crying may seem a little noisy and unsophisticated compared to speaking, but it's your first means of communication. Within days of your birth, your mum could recognise the special sound of your cry, even in a room full of other newborns. And it didn't take her long to get to know the difference between cries for company and those of hunger or discomfort. In fact, if you haven't been fed for some time, just the sound of your hungry cries makes her breasts fill with milk.

CRYING This is the most effective mechanism for communication available to very young infants. Although it is one of many different types of vocalisations that babies can make from the day they are born, crying is the most common and frequent sound they produce in the first six months. During this period, cries represent responses to specific physiological states, such as discomfort, pain, boredom, loneliness, hunger or the need to be changed. Even a baby's very first cry in the delivery room has an important communicative role. It signals to the doctor or midwife that his infant lungs have successfully filled with air for the first time. The nature of early cries can also indicate the presence of problems such as respiratory difficulties, and professionals may use them as indices for assessing the baby's central nervous system.

From the day he is born, your baby's cries are completely unique to him. Very much like fingerprints, they have their own distinctive intonation, pitch, rhythm and intensity. Differences in crying sounds are produced by regulating the amount of air that is being forced through the vocal cords, as well as by varying the patterns of pauses and loudness. Quite amazingly, recordings of babies' cries have demonstrated that these can range across as many as five octaves in pitch.

The individual quality of a baby's cries makes it possible for parents to recognise the sound of their own baby. In maternity wards, mothers are sometimes able to sleep through the sound of other babies crying but wake the moment they hear their own infant. Within a few weeks, parents begin to distinguish between their baby's different cries. In fact, crying is such a successful means of communication that siblings as young as seven can 'read' the meaning of their baby brother's or sister's cries. Interestingly, newborns also seem to pay special attention to the meaningfulness of crying: very young infants often start to cry themselves when they hear the crying of other newborns. This is not so much imitation as a response to the arousal that this arresting noise causes. Moreover, if a tearful newborn hears his own cry played back to him, he will stop crying to attend to this intriguing sound.

Although we are all acutely aware of the emotions aroused by hearing our baby crying – be it anxiety, sadness, frustration or even anger – the sound actually results in specific physiological responses in us. For instance, hearing your little one cry can raise your blood pressure or speed up your heart rate. Furthermore, the parent's type and level of reaction differs as a function of the meaning of each type of cry. This may explain why parents often rate the effect of hearing cries of hunger and pain as more stressful, upsetting or aggravating than, say, those of boredom.

THE VOCABULARY OF CRYING

People who don't themselves have children are often astonished at how well parents seem to be able to interpret their baby's cries. How can they tell that their baby needs to be fed rather than changed, or just needs a cuddle? The secret lies in listening to the clues given by the baby himself, for each baby has a repertoire of different cries signalling specific needs. Studies have shown that the hunger cry is often very rhythmic, has a braying quality and is commonly accompanied by rhythmic movements such as kicking. In contrast, cries of boredom are less regular and coordinated, and may have longer pauses as the baby stops and waits for the desired response. Cries of pain are much more intense than other cries, and signal urgency to the listener. In addition, as the baby grows and tests out an increasingly large range of sounds, parents may start to distinguish distinct vowel sounds in their infant's cries.

If we could hear this baby's cries, we'd be able to tell if she was hungry, bored or in pain.

From the first moments after birth, parents develop their own repertoire of responses to their baby crying. This includes feeding, picking up, cuddling, talking, nappy-changing and, usually when the baby has been put to bed, a wait-and-see-if-baby-will-stop-by-himself response! Their greatest concern is to soothe the distressed baby, but this isn't always straightforward. Instinct is often the only way forwards, but it can be very frustrating for parents to find themselves having to run through a whole range of responses each time their baby cries. Picking up is usually the most successful initial response to crying. Then, if baby is not signalling that he is hungry or needs changing, auditory stimulation such as talking to him or playing music will often be the most calming. During the first few weeks after birth, babies can find white noise very soothing (such as the sound of an untuned television or radio or the rhythmic noise from a washing machine). Such sounds are thought to be comparable to the sounds the foetus experienced in the womb. After a few months of life in the outside world, however, the sound of mum's voice is much more effective, as is the general distraction of a toy or watching a mobile rotate slowly above the cot.

The challenge for parents stems from the fact that the nature of crying progressively changes and is very much a function of the baby's age and developmental stage. While one set of strategies may work wonders for the first few weeks, after a few months your baby will be looking for a very different response to a specific cry than the one you are offering him. Parents can spend weeks learning to respond to different cries, only for everything to change the minute they have cracked the code! At whichever age, a prompt response is better than ignoring a cry. This has been repeatedly shown to be the case. Some parents, and indeed some researchers, have argued that reacting too eagerly to crying can make for a spoilt or manipulative child. But in fact, research has shown that failure to respond to cries often causes more distressed and intense crying. We must remember that the infant has no other means of successfully communicating his needs or emotional and physical state to us. If you choose to ignore or block out your baby's cry, he can only try harder and cry louder.

On the whole, young babies whose cries are answered quickly are more secure and strongly attached to their parents. Furthermore, they develop and learn to use more varied types of non-crying communication at an earlier age than those whose cries are not responded to promptly. Far from reinforcing a negative behaviour by giving your baby attention when he cries, you are actually letting him know that he has successfully communicated with you, that you are tuned into his needs, are there for him, and that he can rely on you.

COMMUNICATING NEGATIVITY It was long presumed that infant negativity, exhibited through withdrawal behaviour such as gaze aversion, shrinking away from touch, ignoring or fussing, was the product of inappropriate or insensitive parenting. Early research posited the emergence of negativity around six months of age, when it was thought that the baby was able to translate his feelings into voluntary actions. More recently, however, research has revealed that negativity can be identified in infants as young as two or three weeks. Young babies seem regularly to alternate between positive and negative responses in their everyday interactions with mum or dad. It is now thought that rather than illustrating the effects of poor parenting, negative responses are important communicative tools with which the baby can control his social and physical environment.

Crying is the most obvious and common form of negativity, and we have already seen how the baby uses it to maintain a stable environment and to ensure that he is provided with food, care and comfort. The same is true of fussing. This is often interpreted by parents as a sign of baby's 'bad temper', whereas in fact baby may be attempting to communicate negative reactions to some specific event. There are many other, more subtle forms of negativity. For instance, changing position to distance himself from a person, turning his head away, arching or stiffening his back, refusing to return smiles or establish eye contact, handling his clothes or blankets excessively, touching his own face repeatedly, sucking his thumb or fingers or even pushing the person away with his hands or feet, may all be used by the baby to convey his negative feelings towards a situation.

Scientists disagree on how to interpret such behaviour. Some suggest that negativity occurs when baby is faced with 'perceptual overload'. In other words, if the situation is overstimulating for the baby and his senses become overloaded, he will respond by withdrawing or rejecting. While it is the case that babies can sometimes be overwhelmed by a particular experience, experiments have shown that this is not the whole story. It has been possible for researchers to demonstrate that it is the quality, not the quantity, of stimula-

I love all the attention I get from people, but there are times when I find it all too much and refuse to play their games. I wish I could just say no, but the only way I can make them understand is to divert my gaze or pull away angrily. Have I stopped loving them?

Of course not. But not having the words to communicate your wishes can be very frustrating, especially when the adults around you sometimes read the wrong meanings from your actions. You have to convey your negative feelings through body language, which can be as effective as using words. Sometimes it's the only way you can influence how people interact or play with you, and in that sense, you're not really being negative. You've found a necessary and productive way of communicating for the time being.

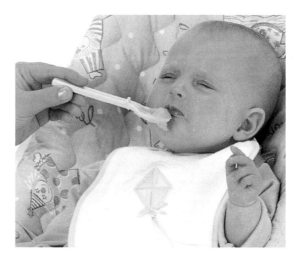

This baby is too young to be able to tell his mum he doesn't like the taste of this new baby food, so he communicates his feelings in the only way he knows: by clamping shut his mouth, screwing up his face and, in a moment, pushing away the spoon.

When a baby's nerves become jangled through overstimulation, she is likely to turn her head away from the source of the stimulation and start to cry, signalling to her parent that it is time to stop the game.

tion that influences the baby's responses. For instance, in one experiment two-month-old babies were encouraged to watch and respond to video images of their mothers. The babies were seated in front of the screen with the researcher, while the mothers were hidden from view and videotaped. Mothers were able to see their child's reactions and asked to respond either appropriately or inappropriately. In the first trial, the mother's image reacted appropriately to the baby's changing facial expressions, vocalisations and gestures while the baby watched her on the screen. In the second trial, the mother was asked to respond inappropriately or not at all to her baby's interaction. Results showed that when the babies' expectations about their mothers' responses were violated, they demonstrated negative behaviour. At first they turned away from the video image, looked puzzled and frowned. They would yawn, fiddle with their clothes and touch their own faces, and finally, as they grew increasingly frustrated, they would often begin fussing. Intriguingly, such reactions are not seen in situations where mother–child interaction is more naturally interrupted. For example, if you were in the middle of playing with your baby when a friend walked in and as a result you stopped responding to your infant for a while, he would not find this surprising and therefore not automatically respond negatively.

So even very young babies are sensitive to the special rules of social interaction. Negativity can be caused by the frustration a baby feels when any of his expectations are violated. If his environment becomes incomprehensible, he is likely to respond by withdrawal, then become distracted and reject the stimulus. Babies may also react negatively when they find themselves incapable of conveying their wishes correctly. Generally, this sort of behaviour involves non-social things, such as experiencing discomfort or tiredness but not being able to convey this appropriately to the parent.

What is interesting is that in interacting with babies, we often unknowingly impose the label of negativity upon infant behaviour, which can unfortunately steer the direction of the subsequent exchange. Observations of mother–baby interaction in a natural setting have demonstrated that up to 20 per cent of a baby's utterances or responses were interpreted by his mother as negative. Common remarks made by the mother included: 'You're tired of this game, aren't you?' or 'You don't want to smile at Mummy, do you?' It seems, therefore, that each mother was translating her baby's inattention negatively, when in fact it was often the case that baby was simply busy exploring his environment, *not* rejecting his mother's efforts to interact.

EYE CONTACT AND EARLY 'DIALOGUES'

Conversations between babies and the people who fill their world starts well before infants begin to understand or produce real language. Parents and visitors make eye contact and instinctively talk to babies whenever they share a moment together. In response, infants make agitated movements, gurgle, smile or simply gaze intently into the person's eyes. Newborns can be observed regularly synchronising their limb movements to the rhythm of the speech directed at them. At first, the actual words used by adults in these early dialogues are largely incidental: infants follow the exchanges mainly on the basis of the person's intonation patterns, the rhythm of the speech, and the accompanying hand gestures and eye contact. However, with time, the sounds of the specific words occurring most frequently become familiar, and this will often determine the baby's attempts at first words.

Crying represents one-way communication from the baby to the parent. However, from the moment they are born, babies take part in various forms of two-way interactions with those around them. The earliest exchanges involve eye contact. This is most noticeable during intimate moments of cuddling and feeding, and elicits other social responses from both parties. Emotions are awakened, closeness is enhanced, and the parent will begin talking to the infant to initiate further exchanges. By four weeks of age, the baby begins to gurgle in response to his parents' vocalisations and soon develops his own repertoire of vocal sounds in imitation of what he is hearing.

Babies actively study the way their parents' sounds and mouth movements go together. Research has shown that if young infants are shown two faces, one mouthing the sound 'ee' and the other the sound 'oo', they will look longer at the face that corresponds with the sound heard through a loudspeaker. In other words they can match facial speech to sound. Other research

Whenever I look into my parents' eyes, they begin speaking to me enthusiastically, even though they know I can't understand a word they're saying! I really enjoy these 'chats', but the only way I can show my appreciation is to kick my feet and pull silly faces at them. Will they think I'm rude or can they understand what I'm doing?

Your parents know you're not being rude, and the way you respond when they speak gives them as much pleasure as any words you can say. It doesn't matter what form the dialogue takes. What is important is the exchange that occurs when you react to their words — making eye contact, kicking your legs, gurgling, making faces or just pausing between gulps when you are feeding. These responses represent your side of the conversation, and they encourage your mum and dad to continue speaking to you.

Long before babies can speak, they can take part in 'conversations' by gurgling happily and kicking their legs in response to their parents' words.

has demonstrated that infants show distress if the sounds produced by the parent on a television monitor don't match the shape of the parent's mouth. Infants also gradually learn to expect certain specific words from their parents in response to specific situations. This hails the beginning of matching words to objects or events. But most interesting for dialogue, babies are also aware of the patterns of turn-taking between their parent's speech and their own kicking or cooing. Studies have revealed that babies show real confusion if the parent's dialogue is not in synchrony with their own vocalisations or movements (that is, if the parent talks through the baby's kicking, or leaves too long before beginning to talk again).

Early pre-speech dialogue between adults and infants shares many qualities with later language behaviour. The most fundamental characteristic of such exchanges is their turn-taking nature. One party is active while the other is quiet, then the sequence is reversed. And, just like conversations, early interaction episodes are unique, following different patterns each time, with peaks of excitement, vocalisation and movements, interspersed by quiet pauses. Each party pays close attention to the other's response and reacts appropriately. But in this case, individual responses are designed to keep the interaction going. Unlike the parent's reaction to the baby's hunger cry, which is generated by a need and has a predetermined structure, the direction and development of a pre-speech dialogue is created by the particular flow of each situation between the two parties in the dialogue. The baby may slowly build up his responses to a crescendo, then go quiet and wait to see what mum or dad will do next. The parent, in return, will react with more and more enthusiasm, mimic the baby's facial expressions as well as his quiet times, and instigate a new cycle of excited dialogue. These early, non-linguistic 'conversations' lay the foundations for human interaction and turn-taking in what will later become real dialogues in language. They also give infants a sense of their own capacity to communicate and to be in rhythmic interaction with their parent, particularly if mum or dad responds sensitively to the infant's attempts at turn-taking.

Eye contact is just one way that babies communicate through sight. During the first six months, they learn to follow the direction of their parent's gaze. Although they may not fixate on the same object, they look towards the same area. Around twelve months, the baby can pick out the object itself and gradually learns to establish joint attention with people by looking to and fro between the object and the person being communicated with. This has the specific intention of sharing an experience. Increasingly, babies use a number of different means of communication, enriching pre-linguistic dialogue by combining gestures with sounds, facial expressions and gazing.

Grinning broadly, this two-month-old is engaged in a non-linguistic dialogue, poking her tongue in and out in turn with her mother.

This little girl has long mastered the art of smiling, but she probably reserves her widest, most charming, toothy grins for her parents.

SMILING AND LAUGHING The development of the smile – or a smiling mouth shape, to be more precise – begins during intrauterine life, when fluctuations in the baby's central nervous system cause the corners of his mouth to turn up slightly. Similar mouth movements can be seen in one- and two-week-old babies in response to loud sounds or voices. These involuntary reflexes often occur when the baby is asleep or just about to doze off, giving the impression that he is having a pleasant dream. At this stage, however, a smiling mouth simply represents a muscular response to auditory stimulation, involving only the muscles in the lower face. Curiously, girl infants display this spontaneous smiling reflex twice as many times as boys, though boys have a much stronger startle reflex. The reflex smile

I've developed two new skills that make everyone pay me extra attention. The first is my grin, which I perfected a little while ago. But the other day, as I listened to dad making funny noises, this sound came out of my mouth as I smiled away. What are these uncontrollable noises I made?

You were laughing. It's great fun for you and others around you, and encourages communication. Smiling was the first truly positive social behaviour you learned to employ. Then, as you started to vocalise more and use noises to express yourself, you developed a gurgle that turned into a laugh. Hearing yourself laugh is in itself rewarding, but what you enjoy most is to see the reaction your laughter gets from those around you.

is elicited by both human and non-human sounds. Only later will it become a selective reaction to specific experiences. By the third week, the infant develops a grin-type expression. This response is elicited by voices when he is in an alert and attentive state. He is not yet responding in a truly social way, but his smiling face promotes interaction and closeness with his parents, and therefore serves a very important, though involuntary, social purpose. At the same time, he is developing control of his facial muscles and gradually learning how to produce these 'smiles' in a more voluntary fashion. By four weeks, therefore, the smile is no longer a physical reflex and baby can actively produce a grin. But his smiles remain a reaction to sound or touch stimulation and are not yet a response to other people's smiles.

Although this newborn appears to be smiling, at this young age his expression is probably no more than an involuntary reflex as he sleeps.

Smiling soon develops into an increasingly responsive form of social interaction. At around five or six weeks the baby begins to smile in reaction to certain things or events, such as a particular toy, noise or action by his parent. You may now even notice your baby smile mid-cry if he suddenly sees something he usually smiles at, and then casually slip back into crying the instant the smile is completed. A few weeks later, however, he will begin to smile more selectively. He now prefers to smile at people rather than things. Although selective smiling is a much more social reaction than reflex smiling, at six weeks the baby still doesn't pay attention to a person's tone of voice or facial expression. At this age he is just as likely to smile at an angry or sad face as he is at a happy, smiling one: he grins in response to changes in your mouth shape rather than to the emotions your facial expressions are communicating.

The truly 'social smile' emerges around four months of age. Now the baby smiles in response to others' smiles. He has discovered what smiling really means in the grown-up world and is actively taking part in an exchange of information. He sees you are contented and smiles back to tell you that he feels the same way. Alternatively, he may initiate interaction by smiling at you, encouraging you to respond to him. Soon, he will learn to use different types of smile – with closed lips, bared teeth or open mouth – and will carefully monitor people's reactions to his repertoire of grins. Studies show that adults respond to any type of baby smile by smiling back. However, one particular type of smile – when baby bares his teeth – tends to encourage the adult not only to smile but to vocalise and nod as well. So he learns to use this smile to influence the way people communicate with him. You think you are in control, but actually baby has you under his thumb! By nine months, the infant has become an expert at smiling, using it cleverly as he interacts with different individuals, but saving his broadest grins for his favourite people.

Laughter emerges within a few weeks of the social smile. Although you may notice your baby making laughing-type vocalisations as early as twelve weeks, at this stage he is testing sounds and responses. He will not necessarily 'laugh' at the same thing on different occasions, as laughter has not yet become a selective response. At this stage, it can be rather frustrating for parents who find something that amuses their baby one night only for it to be ignored the next. But this isn't because putting on the silly hat has become boring to baby. It is simply that he cannot yet select laughter as a voluntary response to communicate his excitement or joy. At five months, auditory and tactile stimulation are the best ways to make babies laugh. Later, as laughing becomes a regular part of his interaction with others, watching something amusing, being tickled and playing peek-a-boo predictably elicit laughter.

Laughter, like smiling, fulfils a very important social function. Primarily, it encourages ongoing exchanges between the baby and others. More than this, however, it ensures that whatever caused the laughter in the first place is repeated as the adult is spurred to make the baby laugh again. This sort of repetition is crucial as it gives the baby several opportunities to learn and make predictions about the current experience or stimulus. On the other hand, if you show the baby something he cannot understand at all, he will not laugh and you are unlikely to play this game again. His use of responses such as laughter and smiling thus places important limits on the things with which you choose to entertain him. So in effect, it is he who sets the social agenda to suit his own abilities.

Smiles and laughter arise as a consequence of a complex interpreting process that the baby undertakes when he is faced with novel or arousing stimulation. Arousal first causes the baby to assess whether the stimulus is dangerous. The next step involves trying to make sense of what he is experiencing. Once this is done, the initial state of arousal decreases and the baby responds with a smile or laughter. It is thought that the more arousing the stimulus, the more likely it is to elicit laughter, as long as it is not really dangerous. A baby may be fascinated by the

Initial fear turns to giggles as the baby realises from his father's smiling face that this game is quite safe.

flickerings of a fire, for instance, but will not smile at it because he senses the true danger. Yet laughter can develop from an initial sense of fear. When thrown into the air by dad, for example, baby's first response may be a bit fearful, but on seeing dad smile confidently (and catching him!), baby's fear will turn into a chuckle. This is an important function of what is known as social referencing: the child assesses the parent's reaction as an aid to gauging what his own should be. But the opposite relation can also be seen between fear and laughter. For instance, initially a baby may find the mask his parent is wearing very amusing, but within seconds his little face crumples into a frightened cry.

My arms aren't always long enough to reach my toys. But now I'm six months old I've made an interesting discovery: if I extend my arm and finger towards the thing I want, mum or dad will pick it up for me. Are they reading my mind?

Yes, in a sense they are. At this age, your actions really do speak louder than words! By trying out different ways of attracting your parents' attention, you learn to communicate what you want without speaking. At first many movements are instinctual, but they later become part of your everyday communication. Soon you'll discover that you can also use pointing to share your experiences with others by indicating funny or interesting events.

POINTING This allows babies to exchange information with those around them. It is a social and communicative behaviour. Babies never point when they are alone. Indeed, they will first actively attract your attention before they point, to ensure that their action will be noticed. At around six months, babies begin pointing to objects out of their reach in order to convey specific desires. This form of pointing is called 'instrumental pointing' and represents a very specific and intentional means-to-an-end action. The resulting response from the parent – to pick up the toy and hand it to the baby – is predicted and confirmed. Within a few months, however, you may be perplexed by a new reaction from your baby. When you hand him the toy he was pointing at, he may look displeased or push it away. Your frustrated little one is feeling cross because this time you didn't understand his behaviour. In this case, he was sharing an experience by showing it to you, not asking for something to be given to him.

This so-called 'declarative pointing' emerges around the end of the first year, and marks an important stage of your infant's development. His endeavour to share an experience with you by pointing implies that he has grasped something fundamental about how to communicate beliefs and feelings. Attracting your attention by pointing to the dog he sees walking past may mean something like: 'Look at that dog, isn't it interesting?' This is quite different from instrumental pointing, which might mean: 'I want that ball, please give it to me.' Declarative pointing may also carry other types of message. It can express invitations to interact: 'Let's do this together', or personal feelings: 'I like that!' At this stage, these special forms of pointing enable the baby to communicate quite complex messages.

The use of declarative pointing usually precedes the onset of word use by a few weeks. It often acts as an index of the baby's language comprehension, as he is increasingly able to respond to parents' object-naming by pointing, for instance, at a duck when mum asks where the duck is. Through such pointing and naming games, the baby learns that there is a word for everything he directs his parents' attention to. When he starts uttering his first words, he will regularly use pointing to complete a phrase. For instance, your baby may point at his bare feet and say 'shoes' in order to ask that you put his shoes on for him. Pointing can therefore act as an integral part of early grammar.

How do others communicate with me?

People don't always communicate with me using words. Sometimes it's just enough for them to look at me in a certain way, or to make a certain movement. How come they're so good at 'talking' to me without words?

They are using facial expressions, body language and movements to express themselves. A smile will attract your attention almost as well as language does. And the way mum and dad hold you also communicates their feelings. For example, when mum's in a hurry and you move your legs too much, she can't change your nappy. She may say 'Ooh, what a lovely baby you are,' but she'll also be communicating her irritation to you through the way she handles you. You can pick up on very subtle clues despite your young age.

GESTURES AND FACIAL EXPRESSIONS A significant amount of human communication takes place without words: it comes very naturally to us. We frequently use body language, facial expressions or gestures to add to, and sometimes transform, what we say – or indeed what we don't say. This is especially true when we interact with babies and young children. Pulling faces (sticking out our tongues or making happy and sad faces) is an example of communicating with exaggerated facial expressions. Our main intention is often simply to attract the baby's attention or provide light entertainment, but it is also very important in helping him learn about the subtleties of human interaction.

The newborn attends particularly to the face, hand movements and the patterns of utterances that people (especially mum and dad) direct at him. He listens to the overall sound of language, but doesn't yet pay close attention to actual words, grammar or the tone of voice. It will be some months before he is able correctly to interpret the meaning of specific facial expressions or hand gestures. But in the meantime, these help to capture and hold his attention. Soon he will develop expectations about what interaction should consist of.

I really like the way mum speaks to me, all high-pitched and happy-sounding. It makes me feel special because she doesn't talk to anyone else like that. Her voice changes the second she turns to speak to someone else. Why does she save this voice for me?

Because it is designed to stimulate you. The way she exaggerates and repeats sounds, uses short sentences and makes her voice rise and fall means it is more interesting for you to listen to. As you can't understand her actual words, it also ensures that you enjoy the experience of language right from the start, encouraging you to pay close attention to human communication. She doesn't need to embellish her speech in this way when she talks to others because they already understand the content and the subtle cues of her speech.

MOTHERESE Parents instinctively adjust their speech when they talk to babies or young toddlers. The style of speech they use is generally referred to as 'motherese' or 'baby-talk', and seems to be an automatic response. Experiments have demonstrated that only hours after birth newborns show a preference for motherese over normal talk. However, in the first few days, babies are attracted most strongly to the sounds to which they were exposed in the womb, so the newborn will show the strongest preference for his mother's muffled voice as it sounded in utero, filtered through the amniotic fluid. The attraction towards motherese becomes stronger after two months, and remains an important feature throughout the baby's journey to language acquisition.

Motherese has several unique characteristics that differentiate it from normal speech. Most noticeably, it tends to be high-pitched and uses a much wider range of intonation patterns, often including a rising tone at the end of each sentence. In normal adult speech, our tone usually falls at the end of sentences. A rising tone is more captivating and, combined with the other special features, gives motherese its sing-song quality. This speech style also includes a large number of attention-getters and -holders, such as frequent use of the baby's name, using many questions, prompts, explanatory hand gestures and regular physical contact. Here's an example: 'Jenny! What's little Jenny doing? Cooing is she? Jenny's cooing at Mummy, right!' Generally, this sort of parent–child interaction concentrates on the here and now. The parent refers only to what can be seen, heard or felt at that moment. 'Look Jenny, look what Mummy's doing now. Mummy's stroking kitty.' Short, simple sentences are used, and the speech is relatively slow and rhythmic, with lots of repetitions. 'That's a dog. Yes, a doggie. It's William's doggie. He's a nice doggie.' The parent will also regularly expand on the child's own utterances in order to invite him into a two-way exchange and render the interaction as much like a conversation as possible. If, for example, a toddler points up and says 'Daddy coat. Coat,' his mother might reply 'Yes, that's Daddy's coat. Daddy's gone to work. But Daddy left his coat here. A nice warm coat, a big coat, Daddy's coat.' Interestingly, siblings as young as three can simplify their speech when they talk to a significantly younger baby.

It seems, therefore, that we have a natural predisposition to adapt the way we talk when we are interacting with someone less able than ourselves. It is achieved quite spontaneously and seems to be regulated by feedback from the infant. Parents constantly adjust their speech in relation to the child's responses, to his level of comprehension and, ultimately, to his own language production. As the child gets older and is perceived as understanding a greater number of words, the parent begins to use longer sentences with new structures. But motherese is not designed as a means of teaching the actual vocabulary or the intricacies of grammar to the baby. Rather, it serves to improve comprehension and promote sustained attention between parent and child. The parents' goal is to hold their baby's attention for as long as they can, and be understood as well as possible. In fact, psychologists have discovered that the content (the words and concepts) and the grammar of motherese have little impact on the child's later grammar and vocabulary. Instead, it is by enabling and encouraging the baby to pay attention to, understand and experiment with speaking that these very special qualities influence and speed up the initial stages of language acquisition.

Just how effective is motherese?

Researchers have shown that if an infant can choose between pushing a button on a box that emits motherese or one that emits normal adult conversation, they will opt for motherese. You can try this experiment for yourself by talking to your baby as you would to another adult. Watch his reaction. Is he looking bored or distressed? Now change to exaggerated motherese. Adopt a very sing-song intonation, repeat your words, exaggerate your speech patterns and use lots of hand gestures and facial expressions: 'Look who's here. It's your te...e...ddy! What a ni...i...ce teddy. Hello baby, says teddy. Hello teddy, says baby.' You may feel rather silly, but watch how your baby responds. His interest will probably pick up immediately, and he may even smile in appreciation.

How do I start speaking?

*Now that I'm producing long sounds like
ma-ma-ma-ma-ma and da-da-da-da-da,
mum and dad seem delighted. They act as if
I'm already saying mama and dada, but I've
just learned to get these neat sounds out –
they have no meaning for me yet. Will I one
day speak properly like they do?*

*You will as you get more familiar with the sounds most
common to your mother tongue. Right now, you practise articulating every vocalisation you can, learning
to control your voice, mouth shape and breath, which
are used together to create each language-like sound
you make. This string of vowel-like and consonant-like
sounds is known as babbling and forms a very important part of your speech learning process, even though
it doesn't in itself have any meaning.*

BABBLING Babies can distinguish between speech
and non-speech sounds from birth. During their
time in the womb, they become familiar with the
rise and fall, the rhythms and the sounds of human
speech. Newborns then spend much of their time
listening to their parents' voices, in preparation for
their own sound production.

Between two and three months, the baby begins
cooing in response to his parents' vocalisations. This
involves making sounds in the back of the mouth, but
does not yet represent the beginning of word production. The baby is simply learning to create sounds
at different pitches and exploring what his voice is
capable of doing. Between four and six months, the
variety of vocalisations he makes increases significantly. He now produces raspberry noises, interrupted by
vowel-like sounds. This clumsy transition between
vowel and consonant utterances is called 'marginal
babbling'. The easier the sound is to produce, the

A GOOD EAR FOR LANGUAGES?

There are some 6,000 languages in the world, constructed around a limited set of special language sounds called
phonemes. These are the sounds that allow one to change
the meaning of, say, 'rice' or 'river' into 'lice' or 'liver'. In
other words, the phonemes /R/ and /L/ change the meanings
of words in English – but they don't, for instance, in Japanese.
Researchers have discovered that, unlike older children and
adults, who generally struggle to learn any new language,
infants up to the age of about ten months can distinguish
between the phonemes of all the languages of the world. But
how do we discover this, given that the babies are too young
to tell us about their capacity? Well, researchers have devised
a simple but ingenious experiment in which babies are placed
in a special seat and wear headphones. They hear one sound
repeatedly until a new sound is introduced. At the point the
new sound is heard, a dancing toy appears on one side. The
baby gradually learns to anticipate the toy any time a new
sound is heard. This is called the 'head-turning' technique.
Researchers first try the sounds of the baby's mother tongue,
and then the sounds of other languages. In Hindi, for example, there are two different /da/ /Da/ sounds which English-
speaking adults only hear as one. Amazingly, infants up to the
age of about nine or ten months can make all these distinctions, whatever their mother tongue. But towards the end of
the first year, they start to lose the capacity to distinguish the
sounds that do not occur in their own language. They will no
longer turn their head when a new sound is introduced. The
English baby will stop turning her head when she hears the
Hindi /da/ replace the other /Da/ sound. So in some ways
young infants have a better linguistic ear than adults.

At seven months old, this little girl has been paying close attention to differences in sounds and mouth shapes and the way they go together.

earlier it appears in the babbling repertoire. From now on, baby's vocalisations begin to take on the elements of the native language. The sounds he doesn't hear very often (those which do not belong to his mother tongue) are produced less and less frequently. So, at the end of the babbling phase, baby no longer discriminates those language sounds not relevant in his day-to-day life.

The next stage of the babbling period involves the use of syllabic structures, from about seven months onwards: baby has learned to go from consonant to vowel and back efficiently. This is seen in long repetitions of sounds such as 'ba-ba-ba', 'da-da-da' or 'ga-ga-ga', and is referred to as 'canonical babbling'. It may not seem very sophisticated to the adult ear, but what the baby is doing is actually introducing some of the rhythmic patterns of vocabulary into his utterances. This is also the stage at which he begins to pay special attention to the sounds and stress patterns most common to the language or languages his parents speak. In the last two months of the first year, his babbling becomes quite complex including variegated sequences such as 'babi' and 'biba'. By now it sounds noticeably different from the babbling of a foreign baby. Babbling is also embellished by gestures, facial expressions, changes in tone of voice, and rise and fall patterns – mimicking many of the qualities of adult speech.

From about eight months onwards, the baby shows comprehension of a limited set of words, although it will be some months before he will *produce* his first recognisable words. He still has quite a lot of practising and learning to do before he's ready to start speaking. Nevertheless, the positive feedback his babbling elicits from his parents is crucial in encouraging him to take the next step towards language production. While babbling carries no meaning, adults react as though they have interpreted and made sense of it: they regularly 'reply' to their infant's babbles with words. A process of mimicking the sounds of the words he hears, perfecting his own speech sounds and observing his parents' reactions leads the baby to begin replacing his babbles with increasingly word-like utterances. These are then gradually transformed and perfected to create distinguishable words.

I've cracked it! My first word: 'Carr'. I can use it to refer to anything I choose – the car, mum's bicycle, even a Frisbee. Mum seems to understand what I mean every time, even though when she talks she uses lots of different words. Will I always use just the one?

No, of course you won't. Producing your first word is already a big accomplishment, but it takes time to learn to control your muscles and pronounce words clearly. The sounds 'kk' and 'aah' are easier than some of the others you've been practising. You've also heard the word 'car' very often. Because you can only say a handful of words right now, you use them to refer to many different things.

FIRST WORDS Babies produce their first conventional words any time between ten and twenty months of age (although rest assured that late word production doesn't necessarily indicate a late developer). Word *comprehension* generally progresses at a fast rate from eight months onwards, independently of a child's attempts to speak. A baby's first words tend to refer to objects or experiences with which he is most familiar – favourite people (mama, dada, himself) or objects (teddy, car), as well as common regulatory words such as 'no' or 'more'. Parents often react to their child's first words by instigating naming games, which act as a reward and reinforce his language learning.

Once the first word or words are uttered, however, parents may find that their infant speaks only in certain contexts. Even the most enthusiastic prompts may fail to result in your baby showing off his new abilities. But this refusal to produce words on cue is not caused by stubbornness: there are several reasons why he may choose to produce a word in one situation and not in another. Earlier words are easier to pronounce than other words which the baby knows but does not yet use. Early words are also context-bound. That is, they are learned as part of an experience as a whole.

More often than not, a single word at this stage refers to an entire situation rather than simply to a specific object. For example, a baby may look at his mother and say 'car' when he sees his dad driving off in the car. In this case, his use of the word 'car' describes an action (driving off), the surroundings (up the street and away from the house), and even includes the agent (daddy). He is observing a situation involving a car, but he doesn't yet possess the words to describe it completely, so he actively over-extends the meaning of the word to encompass every aspect of the situation he is calling his mother's attention to. By doing this, he compensates for the limits of his word production abilities. He still has to learn that there is a word for each thing, that words act as individual symbols. But from the positive feedback his parents give him whenever he speaks, he feels confident that the full intentions of his utterance are being understood.

Single words are also used to refer to categories at this early stage of language production. The word 'car' may thus represent all things with a motor, or all things with wheels. It may even include objects that can act as symbols for related actions. So, for *playing* at driving the infant might choose a Frisbee or plate (to represent a steering wheel) or his pram (a vehicle). He may indicate to you the meaning of the symbol by saying 'Carr' as he picks up the Frisbee, and then add his own sound effects (the 'brrrr' of a motor or the beep of a horn) as he zooms across the room steering around the obstacles in his way with his Frisbee.

Enhancing your infant's language skills

From around twelve months onwards, activities such as looking at picture books with your baby or playing naming games, with objects around the room for instance, can help to stimulate your baby's language development. At first, you will find that you end up performing both sides of the game: prompting 'What's that?' and then naming the object yourself. Even though she may not at first seem to take part, and probably won't initially produce words in response to your efforts, it is still a very interesting activity for your baby –

she will be internally processing what she hears. Bear in mind that your baby can understand many words some time before she can speak them. Be very patient with your child when she begins to utter her first words. This is not the time to correct her pronunciation or to restrict word use to the appropriate object. Instead, interpret her speech by using her other cues such as pointing or following the direction of her gaze, and show her that she has been successful in her communication. Positive reinforcement from you will encourage your baby to make more communicative efforts.

Initially, word production progresses very slowly, with the toddler uttering at most a few new words a month. These first words often include phonetic simplifications – the baby might reduce a cluster of difficult consonants to make just one, more manageable, sound. The word 'smile' might therefore be pronounced as 'mile', or 'strong' as 'song'. Another strategy is

LANGUAGE AND THE BRAIN

Scientists used to think that language (in right-handed individuals) was processed entirely by the left hemisphere of the brain while visual stimuli were processed in the right. We now know that this was far too simplistic. Both hemispheres contribute to language processing (and to complex visual stimuli) throughout life, although the dominance of one hemisphere over the other in different aspects of language processing changes with age. Initially, both hemispheres seem to be involved in many different aspects of language. Over time, however, different parts of the left hemisphere become more specialised for grammar- and vocabulary-learning, although the right hemisphere continues to play some role. Scientists once believed that grammar was processed by Broca's area in the front part of the left hemisphere close to the motor cortex, while vocabulary was located in Wernicke's area in the posterior portions of the left hemisphere, close to the visual cortex. However, as we learn more about the complexities of language-processing in the brain, the role and even the precise volume of these two areas has now become hotly debated.

During a child's development, the right hemisphere takes over the processing of the more social aspects of language, such as narratives, jokes, familiar everyday phrases, and some aspects of intonation that convey nuances of meaning. Adults who have suffered damage to the right hemisphere of the brain sometimes speak with a rather atypical, flat intonation, and often take everything they hear literally, without understanding the subtleties of language. Particularly in the initial years of life, the brain is very 'plastic' – it can restructure itself in response to damage. So, infants requiring a brain hemispherectomy (the removal of one hemisphere) early in life, due to extensive bleeding or other damage, still manage to learn language almost faultlessly with only a single hemisphere: the functions of the removed hemisphere are taken over by the remaining one.

What has become clear is that very complex pathways interconnecting numerous areas of the brain are involved in language comprehension and production and that these develop progressively over the first years of life. In general it is thought that the motor and premotor frontal cortex is involved in verbal fluency, the anterior prefrontal cortex in verbal planning and regulation, Broca's area in expressive speech, the superior temporal and to some extent inferior parietal cortex in the reception of spoken language, the middle and inferior temporal cortex in auditory-visual integration like lipreading for speech output, and the hippocampus, deep within the brain, in the understanding of jokes and sarcasm. All these areas are connected to each other and other areas of the brain, so language and cognitive development are intricately interrelated. The full story must await the results of further neuroscientific research, but it will surely involve complex, dynamic interactions between many parts of the brain.

to use the same consonant throughout a single word: 'doggie' then becomes 'doddie'. Alternatively, the infant may abbreviate long words to partial words, using stress as a cue to select the most pronounced parts of the word. So, 'banana' may be shortened to 'nana', or 'giraffe' to 'raffe' (but never to 'gir').

Babies often stumble awkwardly through the first stage of word production. The step from babbling to uttering distinguishable words is by no means straightforward. Controlling the vocal apparatus to produce clusters of consonants, or to change smoothly from consonant to vowel and back involves very precise manipulation of a large number of muscles. It may take weeks for the infant to perfect the pronunciation of words they have already been using daily. It is important for you to be patient and to recall that at every stage of language acquisition, comprehension exceeds word production. In fact, your child may understand whole sentences before he even begins to utter a single word.

THE NAMING EXPLOSION   Some months after producing his first words, the infant enters a phase of rapid word-learning. The timing of this naming explosion varies significantly, though it often occurs around eighteen to thirty months. While it is quite a noticeable and dramatic development in many infants, others progress more subtly and may even seem to integrate rapid word-learning with word-combining and word-creation (*see pages 104–6*). Researchers believe that several fundamental cognitive changes – changes in the way the infant makes sense of the world – are responsible for the onset of rapid word-learning.

Before he can begin to produce new words at a rapid rate, the infant must learn to decontextualise words. This means that he has to grasp the idea that words are symbols referring to specific entities in the world. So, rather than acting as a name he can use to describe entire situations, categories or experiences, the word 'car' is a label referring to a particular type of vehicle. This may seem quite obvious to us, but consider the following. When you hold up a toy to your toddler and say 'teddy bear' while pointing to it, is there any reason why he shouldn't understand the word to mean 'I am holding up a teddy bear, and showing it to you', or even just 'brown' or 'furry'? We take it for granted that the word is a label for the object we hold, but this is something the child needs to learn. And it doesn't simply involve understanding that everything has a

After struggling with a handful of words for months, I can suddenly produce lots of new words each week. It's as if something has clicked and I can now remember the names of all sorts of things. What is this sudden spurt all about?

Following many months of learning to get to grips with the meaning and sound of words, you've come to understand that there is a name for everything around you. You've also gained increasing control over the muscles responsible for producing words. Now you're ready to expand your vocabulary. Instead of relying on one or two words to describe what you are seeing or feeling, you can use a growing number of words. This is the second stage of learning to speak – but you still have a long way to go before you begin to speak in phrases or sentences.

name and that one word stands for one object. He also has to realise that the same word can apply to a whole category of similar kinds of objects in all sorts of different situations: so the word 'dog' might apply to an alsatian running in the park, a poodle sitting on a carpet, and a labrador play-fighting. This understanding is linked to the development of object categorisation (*pages 179–80*), which assists the child in expanding his vocabulary, as he is now able to segment an event into its different components – people, objects, actions and settings. Once a situation is divided into parts, it becomes easier to learn the names of all these different parts. Expanding memory may also play a role.

Studies have shown that as infants learn new words, they are particularly sensitive to the other cues adults use to communicate their intent. In one experiment, a researcher held up an object the baby had never seen before and, while looking back and forth between the toy and the child, named it several times using a word new to the baby. In this case the baby was able to learn the new word quite easily. However, when the experiment was repeated with the researcher looking at a bucket on the floor instead of the object being named, the baby was more likely to attribute the label to the bucket or what was inside it. The location of the researcher's attention therefore had great bearing on how the child interpreted the new word. Simply hearing it many times did not lead to learning it correctly. So children pay attention to the communicative intention of the speaker, not just to the words that are uttered.

How do I learn more than one language?

I have a friend who speaks English at play school but switches to another language I don't recognise when he talks to his mum. Learning to speak one language is difficult enough. Is he smarter than the rest of us?

No, you're just as clever as he is. Your friend is bilingual – he's learning two languages simultaneously. Because he is relatively new to all speech, it's much easier for him to do this now than when he is older. You too would find it quite easy to pick up different languages at the moment, whereas your parents would have difficulty managing the grammar and accents of new languages because they have become so specialised in the sounds, rules and rhythms of their own tongue.

BILINGUALISM Learning about language is one of the most exciting challenges the human baby faces during early childhood. Spoken language contains complex, highly encoded information. The different elements involved in conveying meaning overlap each other and must be decoded. The task of acquiring language therefore involves breaking the flow of speech into smaller units that can be organised, made sense of and remembered. This is no simple job for a baby. There are no hard and fast rules about how to know where one word ends and the next begins. Adults use subtle cues of intonation, stress and pauses to distinguish word boundaries. But we shouldn't take this ability for granted. Decoding speech begins with the task of segmenting it into dis-

Bringing up a bilingual child

If you speak more than one language at home, or your home language is different from the one spoken at your child's nursery school, your child will effortlessly grow up bilingual. However, if you and your partner do speak different languages at home, it is important for each of you to concentrate on your own native tongue when addressing your infant. This is because he needs to link each language with a specific speaker. If you alternate between languages when talking to your youngster, he may come to think that in one specific situation an object is referred to with a French word, say, while in another situation the same object has to be referred to with an English word – which is obviously very muddling for him. It is fine for you to speak to your partner in a different language, because you are not using motherese or directly addressing your child. But once you turn to your baby, you should regularly each use one language. Remember, too, that languages don't just differ in the way they use specific words to refer to things: they also differ in grammar. So, if your child is simultaneously learning English and German, you are entitled to be very impressed by the grammatical differences he is gradually mastering. For example, in English we might say: 'Tomorrow I would like to go to the park', but to say the same thing with German word order, we would have to say something like: 'Tomorrow would I to the park to go like'. If an infant grows up bilingually, this poses no problem, whereas an adult learning a second language may find such changes in word order almost insurmountable. So sometimes toddlers are smarter than adults!

tinct parts. Interestingly, linguistic rhythms such as phrasing are not restricted to human communication. Research has shown that phrase-type structures can be identified in the sound productions of primates, as well as in whale songs. Even the grooming movements that mice use to communicate with each other can be divided into recognisable and clearly meaningful segments.

At around six months, infants attend to clauses: the part of sentences that includes the subject and conveys the intent of the utterance. For instance, infants are capable of discriminating good clause boundaries from bad ones. So if a researcher places a pause in the wrong place – 'the boy who…walked along the…road is tired' – infants will react differently from when pauses are in the right place – 'the boy…who walked along the road…is tired'. By nine months, they begin to distinguish phrase units – 'the boy/is walking'. This is the time when babbling takes on rhythms resembling phrases, perhaps with rising intonation at the end. Finally, by around eleven months, they attend to even smaller units, and segment speech into individual words. Thus, babies face the language challenge by working from the general to the detail, with each new level of language acquisition influencing the next. But the cues used to decode language are not the same in each language.

LEARNING A SIGN LANGUAGE

Babies born to deaf parents present an especially fascinating case to researchers investigating the acquisition of language, for although they're not often exposed to spoken language, they do of course experience linguistic communication in the form of sign language. Those of us who have not had any experience of signing may look upon it as a repertoire of hand movements representing variations of the gestures we use in our own everyday lives. Far from this being the case, sign languages are actually rich in vocabulary and subtle shades of meaning conveyed through complex grammar. They also include the use of metaphors, the equivalent of rhyming, and slang – just like any spoken language. You can even 'whisper' in sign by making your manual movements low down on your lap and smaller than usual. Furthermore, while English and American spoken languages, for example, are very similar, British Sign Language differs significantly from American Sign Language. In fact, they are as distinct from each other as French and Russian.

Intriguingly, studies have indicated that the babies of deaf parents learn sign language by going through similar stages to those learning spoken language. Their first experience of signing involves exposure to motherese-type variations of normal signs: deaf parents exaggerate their hand shapes and movements, repeat words and phrases, and use body language, exaggerated facial expressions and vocalisations to improve comprehension. In return, their infants begin by 'babbling' in sign: trying out segments and patterns of hand movements. Research has shown that in doing so, babies try out a whole range of possible hand shapes and movements before narrowing them down to those signs which are relevant to the sign language used by their parents. This is similar to the way babies with normal hearing, or 'hearing babies', born to non-deaf parents babble every sound from every language before concentrating on those of their native tongue (*see boxed feature on page 94*). Babies learning a sign language also go through a spoken babbling phase, but congenitally deaf infants give this up at around eight or nine months in favour of continuing to develop signs, probably because they can't hear their own utterances. Hearing babies of deaf parents grow up 'bilingual' in sign and spoken language because they hear what goes on outside the family environment. They may even act as interpreters for their parents at quite an early age. These children switch from sign to speech as easily as a bilingual child might switch between Swedish and French.

As early as eight months, babies learning to sign progress to the next stage: signing single words – generally object names – but without yet using any grammar. These first proper signs tend to occur earlier than the first words spoken by hearing infants (usually any time between ten and twenty months) because making discernible and correct manual signs seems initially to require less muscular control than producing speech.

In the few months after the emergence of single-word signs, the infant begins trying out different word combinations. Throughout these early signing phases, babies may also make use of additional communication skills, using head movements as well as signs. Finally, becoming fully conversant in signing involves learning about the complexities of the native sign language of the parent. This includes employing the correct grammar – such as the use of pronouns, and past, present, and future tenses for verbs – as well as using movement stresses to convey intonation.

Interestingly, babies who are born deaf of hearing parents and who lack regular early contact with native signers show an amazing compulsion to develop their own sign language. They compensate for the lack of proper sign language stimulation by making up sign words and even short sentences in order to express their thoughts, intentions and desires. Although this made-up language does not achieve the complex levels of vocabulary or grammar seen in real sign languages, it nonetheless goes well beyond rudimentary gestures and pantomime-type communication, and beautifully illustrates the human drive for language.

This toddler has just learned the word for 'nose'.

Every different language is characterised by its own linguistic rhythm. For instance, in English stress is the most apparent and obvious cue for segmenting speech. We say, for example, 'giráffe' not 'gíraffe', and we distinguish the noun 'cóntrast' from the verb 'to contrást'. The French language uses a different system: syllable units are the main cues to segmentation and stress is evenly placed across every syllable in a word. A common question asked by parents, therefore, is whether speaking to babies in a number of different languages confuses them, putting obstacles in the way of smooth language acquisition.

Scientists are divided over this issue. However, evidence indicates that it is possible to use a linguistic rhythm learned in one language to decode other languages. Most children in the world today grow up bilingual or even multilingual. As we discussed earlier, young babies have a unique ability to distinguish all the sounds of every human language before they start to specialise in those of their native language or languages (*page 94*). Therefore, the younger a child experiences a variety of different languages, the easier it is for him to become proficient in them. Parents are therefore advised to make a concerted effort to speak to their babies in different languages if more than one is spoken at home. Your infant may have double the number of words to learn if he is growing up bilingual, but this will not slow him down. He will go through the same stages of language acquisition regardless of the fact that he is learning more than one language. He may at times alternate between both languages, but he will still find it a lot easier to learn two languages now than he will later in life.

LOOKING AHEAD **While your child now has an impressive vocabulary, he still has some way to go on the road to adult language – he needs to develop a rudimentary understanding of grammar before he can convey any meaning beyond single words. But once he has acquired a critical number of words, he will start to combine them to produce his first sentences. He may also begin to mimic the words of those around him, repeating everything you or his older siblings say. This can be maddening, but he isn't doing it to annoy you: the more complex sentences supplied by others help him to analyse the structure of language. Although your infant may begin to hold increasingly sophisticated dialogues with you, however, you may notice that he is still quite tongue-tied when it comes to interacting with his little playmates. Becoming a competent conversationalist with peers takes longer.**

Today I saw dad tidying up the kitchen with the broom. I went to tell mum about it, but I wasn't sure how, so I said: 'Daddy brooming'. This made her laugh. Did I say something wrong?

Well, you applied the rules of language in a very creative way. You already knew the noun 'broom', but you weren't familiar with the verb 'to sweep'. So, to convey your dad's action, you added '-ing' to broom, making a new word. It's very clever. In fact you followed the same principles as the ones used to make conventional words in the English language. There's no reason why there shouldn't be a verb 'to broom'! This stage of experimenting with words and grammar is important and helps you master all the difficult rules of language.

WORD COMBINING Once a child has learned around 100–150 words, he will begin putting them together to create short phrases. This may occur any time between eighteen and thirty months. Initially, these phrases often include two or three nouns (such as 'daddy shoe'). The toddler will concentrate on using words that carry most meaning, omitting less essential words such as 'the' or 'but'. Yet adding just two words together allows the toddler to convey a surprising amount of information. Remember how, in the previous phases of language acquisition, one word often referred to whole situations? This left parents with a rather difficult interpreting task. The ability to string two or three words together greatly narrows the focus of the child's utterance. He is now able to direct your attention far more easily to the experience he is trying to share with you.

Soon after the onset of word combining, you will begin to notice the emergence of clear grammatical rules in your toddler's speech as he begins to experiment and conform to the principal conventions of language. This can be a fascinating and enchanting time for parents, as their little ones make charming but ingenious mistakes in their speech.

Grammar is among the hardest aspects of language to learn. One of the first rules children seem to grasp is the addition of 's' to indicate plural. This might seem easy enough to us. But we take for granted the knowledge that 'one goose' does not become many 'gooses', and that the word 'mice' and not 'mouses' is the plural of 'mouse'. These exceptions to the rule appear quite arbitrarily in our language, and certainly confuse matters for the child. An enlightening example of the intricacy of the English language was given by the mother of one little girl. After several weeks of correctly producing the phrase 'my nose', upon discovering the plural marker the child temporarily began calling it 'my noe' because she wished to convey that she only had one nose! (Just think about the relation between 'toe' and 'toes' versus 'nose' and 'noses'! Or 'an elephant' – is it 'a nelephant'? We really present our infants with some tricky linguistic puzzles!)

At the single word level, an expression such as 'all-gone' might be used to express the fact that the child has eaten all his food. But later, he begins to combine 'all-gone' with other words in his existing vocabulary to express a variety of meanings. So 'all-gone daddy' might mean that dad has gone to work; 'all-gone dog' indicates the dog has run away; 'all-gone bath' as the bath is emptied; 'all-gone nappy' (as dad changes the child); and 'all-gone mummy eye' as (mum closes her eyes).

Other so-called 'pivot words' appear as a function of the child's linguistic experience. So if parents often say 'do you want some more?', the toddler may use 'more' as a pivot in his early grammar. Combinations like the following tend to appear: 'more bath' (I want more water in the bath); 'more bird up' (there's another bird flying by), and 'more daddy peepo' (I want daddy to play hide and seek again).

Toddlers will also vary word order to convey different meanings. So, for example, 'sock mummy' might mean that the child wants his mother to put his sock on, but 'mummy sock' (the same two words in a different order) might mean 'I saw the cat playing with mummy's stockings!' Gradually the child starts to introduce other grammatical markers of his mother tongue, so 'all-gone mummy eye' might become 'mummy's closing eyes', and 'baby toe' plus a pointing action might become 'those my toes'.

The past-tense marker '-ed' is another rule which begins to appear in the child's early speech experimentation phase. This is an exciting discovery for the infant. For the first time, he is able to refer not only to the here and now – which has been the main focus of interaction up to this point. The ability to use the past tense adds a new dimension to his speech. He can now tell people about things that only he saw, for instance. Again, mistakes are easily and understandingly made. Toddlers who have been correctly using, say, 'came' and 'went' may suddenly (and temporarily) start to use 'comed' and 'goed' or 'wented'. Why is this? They

'Mummy, juice.' With only a limited vocabulary available to him at first, the toddler will combine his utterances with gestures in order to convey complex meaning.

seem to have discovered that the ending '-ed', from verbs like walked, looked, watched and lifted, all take '-ed' when referring to the past, so they extend this to all the verbs they use. That's why some come out as 'goed' or 'hitted'. But you can see how these so-called errors are actually signs of your child's intelligence in analysing the rules of English.

I've been getting better at this speaking business, and seem to find it quite easy to make myself understood by grown-ups. But I find myself all tongue-tied when it comes to chatting to my little friends at nursery school. Why do I find it more difficult to speak to other toddlers than adults?

The reason you and your little friends have difficulty in communicating smoothly with words is that you are all still novices at the language game. When you talk to mum or dad, they are able to fill in the gaps when you get stuck, and you can carry on knowing that they understand you. You've learned that adults are rather good at making sense of your speaking attempts. Your friends, on the other hand, share all your own difficulties with language and this makes it hard for you to know just what they have understood of what you've said. As a result, starting up such conversations and maintaining them can be complicated and often frustrating.

BEGINNING TO TALK WITH PEERS The transition from parent–child to child–child interaction is by no means an easy step for toddlers. The early interactive exchanges infants experience are usually initiated, guided and encouraged by adults who have the ability to take the lead and guarantee some level of mutual comprehension. Parents are generally really good at interpreting the gestures, actions, facial expressions and utterances made by the toddler, and their careful interpretation efforts provide a sort of scaffold upon which mutual understanding can be built. Then, as the child gets better at taking part in the language dialogue, so the parent withdraws some of his or her support, encouraging the child to try to get his message across alone. This serves not only to promote self-confidence in the toddler, but boosts further learning and motivates the child increasingly to engage in conversation. A successful balance in what the adult and child contribute to the conversation is constantly updated as the child develops.

Early spoken interaction with peers is dramatically different from the carefully adjusted parent–child discourse. It requires many additional skills that toddlers do not at first possess. This is why you will notice a substantial delay between the stage at which your child begins to speak with you and other adults, and the stage at which he starts really using language to communicate with other toddlers. Adult–child dialogues often begin as early as twelve to eighteen months, while toddler–toddler conversations may not emerge until the latter part of the third year. There is little research documenting the characteristics that distinguish the discourse between toddlers and adults and that between toddlers themselves. What is known is that when talking with peers, young novice conversationalists have great difficulty in establishing what knowledge they can take for granted and what knowledge has to be spelt out to their conversational partner. So a toddler may say, 'Jimmy took it', not explaining that Jimmy is his brother and 'it' is his favourite toy. In other words, the child doesn't predict another's knowledge or comprehension of the situation. Furthermore, young speakers find it particularly hard both to convey and to interpret feedback cues, like frowning or questioning, which would otherwise provide vital information about whether the message had indeed been understood.

As a result of these obstacles, early child–child conversations are often very egocentric: they are more like joint monologues than dialogue! Each youngster will take his turn in delivering some sort of monologue, usually concerning something relevant to the current context (the game being played, the room, toys, people around), but this will not necessarily be a shared topic of conversation. The toddler will rely very much on various aspects of the physical setting in which the 'conversation' is taking place. In effect, then, toddlers will seek shared situations rather than shared knowledge in order to establish and maintain some degree of shared understanding.

A special language? Twins often develop a particular way of speaking to each other which only they can understand.

It is clear the toddler–toddler discourse presents a special challenge to the developing child. It fails to provide him with some of the vital support that an adult can offer in language production. In fact, research shows that infants who spend more time communicating with peers and other children than with adults acquire language more slowly. They may even develop slight language disorders, although these are usually only temporary. A special case of this is twins, who often interact with each other at least as much or to a greater extent than with adults. They often develop a special way of speaking to each other, and this 'twin language' is usually characterised by serious mispronunciations that sometimes render the speech unintelligible to anyone else. It has been found that twins are commonly slower in acquiring language because they spend so much time interacting with one another without being able to provide the kind of language support that an adult could. Twin language is not a real language, however. Usually it involves mispronunciations that get exaggerated with time because the two understand one another; research suggests twins do not create a new grammar.

Learning to Move Around

There are two forms of motor development — gross motor development (the subject of this chapter) and fine motor development (the subject of the next chapter) — which, combined, eventually transform the infant from a helpless, reflex-driven dependent being into an increasingly independent toddler in control of her motor movements. All parents eagerly await the moment when their baby sits, crawls and takes her first steps, but it is important to recall that children reach developmental milestones at very different ages. Some babies sit and crawl early but don't walk for a frustratingly long time, whereas others may not crawl at all and go straight from sitting to walking. Don't forget, each baby is an individual with a mind of her own and her own priorities about how she progresses!

The first two years of life are unlike any other period in human physical development. Enormous changes in the size, strength and relative proportions of the infant's body take place during this time. Because we take our movements so much for granted, we often forget just how difficult each of the developmental milestones are. Becoming a biped is a long process. If you dangle your newborn's feet on a flat surface and support the rest of her body, she will seem as if she can already walk. This is just a reflex, however. She has a very long way to go before she can support her own weight, and lots of brain pathways need to develop for her to be able to send messages to her limbs to control her movements.

When your baby first comes into the world, she will be uncoordinated and have almost no control over her body. She will also be curled up in the so-called 'foetal position', so her first job will be to stretch out her arms and legs so that they can lie flat. This takes a lot of muscular effort, and she will spend much of her waking time using her cot as an exercise gym, continually moving her arms and legs. The more she moves, the more specialised her brain will become in guiding her neck, head, arm and leg muscles to do what she wants them to do.

Two principles govern the acquisition of motor coordination in human infants. The first is the 'cephalocaudal' principle, which implies that muscular control develops from the top of the body downwards: first the neck, then the upper body and the arms, then the lower trunk and the legs. Thus head control emerges before sitting, and walking is the last to develop. The second is the 'proximo-distal' principle, which states that motor control develops from the centre of the body outwards. So your baby will initially have more control over her arms than her hands. Next she'll learn to direct her closed fists towards objects before she can pick them up. Finally, control will develop in her fingers, enabling her to manipulate tiny objects in new and interesting ways. All these developments go together with the growth of brain pathways that become increasingly specialised in movement control.

So at first your baby will be unable to support the weight of her large head and brain. Learning to control the head and neck is one of the first achievements. This will allow her to look around at the world when she is held up against your shoulder, or to push up and scan her environment if placed on her stomach when awake. Then, one day you will come into your baby's room in the morning and find she has turned over! This new accomplishment means she can now move closer to coveted toys in her cot. You will probably sit her in reclining baby chairs at first, but there will come a time when she is able to hold herself in the seated position for a few seconds. What a thrill — albeit short-lived because she will fall forwards or back very frequently for quite a while. She has to establish and maintain her centre of gravity. Finally, with legs wide apart, and not very lady-like, she will sit unaided and be able to stretch forwards for things within reach.

Researchers have often noted that it is in toppling over from sitting up that many infants land by chance in the crawling position. Sometimes it's good to make mistakes! But, as we mentioned above, not all infants crawl, so don't worry if yours is happy simply to sit and play or maybe to bottom-shuffle along. In fact, scientists often wonder why infants crawl at all. After all, no one teaches them to do this, and they don't see their parents crawling. It just seems that the desire to move around — either by crawling or by walking — is extraordinarily strong.

Curiously, when babies do start to stand and walk, they move more slowly, can only keep up with difficulty, and generally can't get from A to B as easily as they did when they were crawling. Yet becoming a biped is such a powerful drive that, no matter how difficult it seems, you'll see your budding toddler try again and again, full of the joys of her new achievement. From then on, there will be no stopping her.

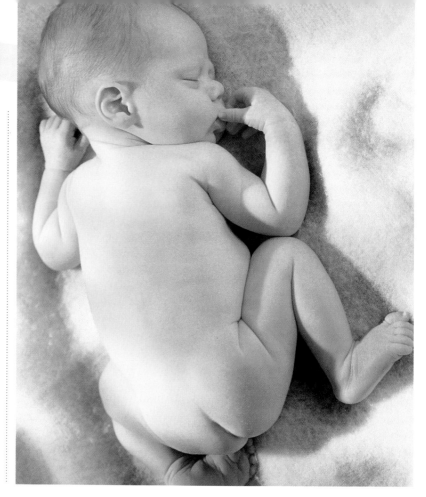

How do I start to control my movements?

When I was inside mum's tummy, I was quite comfortable curled up almost like a ball. But now I'm out, I seem to be stuck in the same position, even though there's much more space to stretch out in. Why can't I straighten my body like everyone else?

For the first few days after birth, you remain in what is known as the 'foetal position', which your body grew used to while you were squashed in the womb. Once you're born, it's quite normal for your limbs to stay bent and close to your body for a little while because your muscles need to strengthen and lengthen before you can stretch out properly. But you won't be like this for long. As you become increasingly active and your movements more vigorous, your limbs will become stronger and heavier and your body will straighten.

GETTING OUT OF THE FOETAL POSITION

Newborn babies spend most of their time asleep, and parents will notice that initially their baby tends to rest all curled up. In the foetal position, the legs and arms are bent inwards under the body when the newborn is lying on her front, or bent in the air and drawn towards the body when she is on her back. This strange-looking body posture is left over from life in the womb and lasts only a matter of days, or weeks at most. It results from the newborn's lack of muscular strength and control over her limbs. No longer restricted by the confining walls of the uterus or effortlessly supported by the amniotic fluid, the baby must now develop stronger muscles and experiment with mobility by making frequent and regular jerky, reflex movements. Your newborn will spend much of her waking time doing little workouts by kicking her legs, flaying her arms and stretching out her whole body in response to internal stimuli, such as the beginning of a yawn, or external stimuli, such as your voice or a moving object. These erratic movements help to build up and elongate her limb muscles, uncurl the lower trunk around the hip and generally stretch out her posture. As the limbs get stronger, they also become heavier and soon come to rest at the sides of her body.

While the foetal position appears to be quite a restrictive body posture, the newborn is actually able to use it to move, albeit involuntarily, from A to B for the very first time. Parents may be baffled to discover that their sleeping, curled-up baby has found her way from the bottom of the cot to the top, even though she generally seems incapable of making any constructive movement. How does she manage this? The newborn is equipped with particularly strong reflexes that allow her successfully to creep up the sheets. Using her grasping reflex to tighten her tiny fingers around folds of material, she hoists herself along the mattress, pushing with her bent legs and feet. It is thought that babies are compelled to move like this so that the top of their heads come into contact with a surface they can rest against. This drive may reflect the baby's memory of feeling her head pressing against the walls of the uterus. She may therefore be seeking reminders of the comforts of life in utero. The newborn may also use her creeping reflex if she is getting overheated under the baby blankets. This is why parents are always advised to lay their baby to sleep towards the lower half of the cot mattress. The creeping reflex disappears by the age of about two months, by which time the baby's limbs have gained significant strength, her legs have straightened and she is beginning to control her movements more effectively.

Human beings are born with all the muscle fibres of their bodies already in place. But it is only the baby's continual movements from the first days of life that lengthen and thicken each muscle as it increases in total mass. At birth, muscles account for only twenty-five per cent of the baby's total weight. By adulthood, this proportion will have almost doubled: more than forty-three per cent of average adult body weight is muscle. Muscle growth is most pronounced during babyhood. While it may not be apparent to impatient parents eagerly awaiting the first time their baby sits, crawls or stands, the first year of life is marked by amazingly fast body growth and increase in overall muscular strength. If you take a person's whole life span into account, these motor milestones are reached at an incredibly fast pace. Never again during your child's life will her physical development progress at such a rate.

Your newborn will rarely keep still when he's awake – flinging his arms and legs about, especially when you're trying to change him! But he isn't trying to be awkward: his constant exercising helps to enhance his muscular control.

My head is so large and heavy, it flops about uncontrollably unless someone supports it for me with their hand. I must have an incredibly huge brain! Why can't I hold my head up proudly on my own?

It's precisely because of your large brain that your head is disproportionately big and heavy at this age. That's why your weak neck muscles aren't yet capable of supporting your head. You're not alone in this. All newborn babies have heads that look out of proportion with the rest of their bodies. It will take several weeks before you are ready to start lifting your head and controlling its movements.

At six weeks, this baby girl lacks the strength to keep her head in line with the rest of her body when she's gently pulled into an upright position.

LIFTING THE HEAD Unlike many other newborn mammals who are able fully to support their heads and even get unsteadily to their feet within minutes of birth, human babies are born almost helpless in terms of mobility. Evolution has given us larger brains in proportion to our bodies than other species, so human children look top heavy throughout the first years of life.

Head control is one of the first important developmental milestones of motor coordination. It is a very gradual process that is not perfected until the latter half of the first year, when the baby is finally able to control and alter her head posture in response to a multitude of subtle auditory and visual cues. At birth, your baby's neck muscles are so weak and the head so heavy that at best she is able to turn her head from side to side when it is supported, and to keep it upright for a brief moment if she is held balanced in an upright position. But at this point, her head will quickly flop forwards on to your shoulder or backwards into your cupped hand.

Any head movement the newborn does make, like turning towards a noise she hears, results from an involuntary reflex at this stage. However, while the neck muscles of your newborn are not strong enough to support the weight of the head when she is lifted from a horizontal to a vertical position, the muscles are nevertheless responding in all the right ways, tensing against the force of gravity. By measuring changes in muscle activity and tension, scientists are able to ascertain which muscle reflexes are actually operative a long time before they are observable to you. So, however floppy your baby's head seems to be, in fact her muscles are responding whenever she is picked up.

The ability to lift and control the head opens up a whole new world for the infant. She can now more actively choose what she looks at and observe things from different angles. These albeit brief glimpses of the world fuel her desire to try to lift her head again. The age at which a baby reaches the different stages of head control varies quite significantly between individual infants. By approximately three weeks (though this ranges from nine days to three months), the baby can hold her head erect, albeit unsteadily, if she is in an upright position: she no longer needs to rely entirely on the support of a cupped hand. By around six or seven weeks, her muscles are strong enough to maintain a stable upright head posture. She soon attempts to lift her head up if she is lying on her front, and achieves steady head control when she turns her head to watch a moving object or locate an

WHY DO NEWBORNS HAVE SO LITTLE CONTROL OVER THEIR BODIES?

Being able to hold your head aloft may seem a simple enough action, but it in fact depends on a number of complex processes in the brain involving connections within and between different areas. These pathways are not present initially. At birth, most motor activity is governed by the sub-cortex in the brain and takes the form of reflex reactions. For more complex actions, connections have to form between the motor cortex and other parts of the brain. By one month, the neurons in the motor cortex are rapidly developing dendrites, which significantly increase the surface area of each neuron so that it can create a greater number of links with other neurons. Neurotransmitters carry electrical impulses from one neuron to another, thereby establishing a synapse between the two. This process of synaptogenesis progressively creates a rich network of connections between areas involved in generating movement: the motor cortex, the cerebellum, and the frontal cortex. As a result, the infant's movements become increasingly voluntary. By four-teen to sixteen weeks, the primary motor areas are well developed, so the baby is able to control the movement of the arms and upper body. But the areas of the brain govern-ing the lower trunk and limbs, as well as those responsible for fine motor movements such as those of the hands and fingers, form connections somewhat later, which is why babies only begin to walk or hold a spoon, for instance, when they are much older.

interesting sound. At two months of age, however, her movements are still not well coordinated, and if she tries to combine lifting up her head and stretch-ing out an arm, she will usually find herself face down on the mattress again!

Babies frequently placed on their stomachs when they are awake and alert often achieve head and neck control a little earlier than those who are used to lying mainly on their backs. This may be due to the fact that babies have a pro-tective reflex to keep their mouths and noses exposed, meaning they turn their heads to one side if they are on their fronts. But the strong drive to attend to what is going on around them soon compels them to lift and turn their heads to investigate a larger portion of their surroundings. Of course, this does not mean that parents should be encouraged to place their baby on her stomach when it's time for sleep. Research clearly shows that sleeping in this position increases the chances of cot death, and babies should always be put in their cots on their backs. It is only when active and alert, and under the constant watch-ful eye of mum or dad, that she should spend time lying on her front.

Although by two and a half months the baby seems to have mastered head movements and control, it is only later that she finally develops the ability to alter her head posture and orientation in response to subtle changes in the environment. For example, while you would automatically keep your head as upright as possible to reduce the disorienting motion of going round a sharp bend in a car or the side-to-side rocking of a boat, small infants are unable to do this. By placing a baby in an experimental room with moving walls, researchers have shown that such a skill takes at least seven months to evolve.

This one-month-old has devel-oped sufficient muscle control to keep her head up, provided she is firmly held in a sitting position by her mum.

How do I change position?

Something amazing happened today. One minute I was lying on my front on the sofa, pushing myself up with my arms, and the next I was lying flat on the carpet, arms and legs in the air. How did I manage to get there all by myself?

You rolled over from your front to your back by accident. You tipped your balance a little too far to one side when you were trying to raise your upper body off the sofa in order to see better, and wound up pushing your whole body over in one go. Sometimes when you combine movements such as pushing, twisting and wiggling, you can change your position completely without any assistance. And now that you've discovered by chance how to roll from your front to your back, you can start to practise rolling over from your back to your front, which is a bit more tricky.

ROLLING OVER This is another important milestone in motor development, enabling the infant to change from one position to a completely different one, or even to get to objects beyond arm's reach. Babies begin rocking from side to side and from back to side some time between two and seven months. Within a month of mastering this rocking motion, the baby will discover how to alter her position even more dramatically by rolling over from front to back or vice versa. It is easier to roll over from the prone position (lying on the stomach) than it is from the supine position (lying on the back), and therefore tends to occur a little earlier. Quite often, the baby will discover this new and exciting skill quite by accident, as the result of an involuntary shift in gravity as she pushes her chest off the ground or mattress to look around the room. Using her arms as levers and possibly rocking at the same time, she will shift her weight a little too far, tip the balance that has kept her steady in this desired position and roll to one side and over on to her back. Though involuntary, such an accidental change of position opens up a whole range of opportunities for the baby: that person she could hear but not see a minute ago is suddenly facing her! She quickly learns to associate her actions with their interesting albeit unplanned outcomes, and then endeavours to roll over from front to back intentionally.

Rolling over from the back to the front rarely happens by mistake. It requires intentionality from the outset. The baby actively strives to achieve this change in posture through much practice and strenuous attempts. By combining a series of

'Here we go!' This eight-month-old has discovered the joys of turning from side to side to get a new view of her surroundings (and a new achievement in the world of mobility).

A workout for your baby

Although babies reach the various motor milestones at their own pace, when their bodies are ready, there are various things you can do to encourage your infant's progress.

From a very young age, experiencing the world from different angles expands your baby's knowledge of her environment: for example, objects alter their apparent shape and size when viewed from changing positions. To give your infant experience of these different views, hold and carry her around the room in various postures – on her stomach, her back, her sides and against your shoulder. Lifting her into the air will also give her thrilling new sensations of the pull of gravity.

There are a number of ways you can guide your baby through a regular workout. When she is lying on her back, take her hands and pull her

slightly, leaving some of the lifting of her head and neck to her own efforts. This strengthens her arm and neck muscles and encourages her progressively to take control of the movement herself. Next, flex her legs and let her press the soles of her feet against the palm of your hand. This exercises her knee and thigh muscles, as well as the pelvic area. If she is alert, turn her over on to her stomach and then call to her or shake a rattle just above her head to spur her to try to lift her head and upper body; this also helps to strengthen the neck and back muscles. Finally, encourage your baby to recognise her potential to roll over by rocking her to and fro and holding her briefly on her side before tipping her gently over. Make these activities enjoyable for your baby by talking to her excitedly about what is happening and congratulating her on each new position.

different actions, she produces sufficient momentum to tip her balance and propel her weight in the desired direction. So, in order to roll over from the supine position, she first has to rock to and fro until she comes to rest on her side, then arch her body backwards, with her head thrown as far back as possible, next twist one leg round and the other under, so as finally to push her upper trunk over on to the front. It is a real accomplishment that uses up quite a lot of energy. But she is rewarded by the knowledge that she has found a new form of mobility: the way she faces when she is lying down is no longer mum or dad's decision.

Interestingly, some babies seem to spend weeks happily rocking to and fro without bothering to roll over completely. Others choose always to roll in one particular direction and not the other, once they master this skill. Most also do their initial 'practising' in private, and cause their parents' hearts to miss a beat by rolling off the changing table out of the blue one day! At this age, infants have no concept or fear of depth and therefore do not perceive the danger of falling off one surface on to another. While it may be lots of fun if she lands on a soft and bouncy surface, rolling over can also lead to all sorts of accidents. So parents should never leave their baby unattended anywhere there may be a risk of falling off an edge. If you are in the habit of taking your baby to bed with you, it is a good idea to place pillows on the floor all around the bed. This provides a soft landing if she happens to roll off the mattress while you're grabbing those precious few hours of sleep.

I can't seem to get the hang of this sitting game! The minute mum takes her hands away or moves the pillows from behind me, I flop over. It makes her laugh, but I don't find it funny because I try really hard to stay upright. What am I doing wrong?

All the progress you've made so far has concentrated on strengthening the muscles in your neck, shoulders and down your spine, so you haven't yet developed the necessary muscle strength and coordination in your lower body to sit alone. After a bit of practice, you won't need the pillows any more, leaving your hands free to explore. But you're in for a few tumbles along the way!

Propped up by cushions, this baby girl gets an interesting new perspective on her world – but she doesn't yet have the power in her back to prevent herself from slowly sliding down in the chair.

SITTING UP With the growing use of baby seats, rocking chairs, and even slings, babies experience the world from a fairly upright and seated-like position from a very young age. However, resting back in a curved seat is not the same as sitting alone. In order to maintain a seated posture, the baby must first be able to hold her head erect and steady unaided, and have good control over the upper trunk. But the prerequisite degree of motor control and strength in the neck, shoulders and spine takes some months to develop.

The very earliest sitting behaviour can be seen at approximately two months, around the time your infant has developed fairly steady head control. At this age, a baby will be happy to be placed in a seated position if she is properly supported on each side and tilted back far enough to prevent her toppling forwards. However, she remains passive in this position; she makes few attempts to move her arms and legs, and is simply content to contemplate her surroundings from this new angle of vision.

By three and a half months, the baby needs less support and may begin making more effort to remain in the seated position. She can now move her arms more easily and her hands are free to hold objects. This is an important discovery. Up to now, she hasn't perceived the full potential of sitting – perhaps because she has been concentrating hard on safely staying put, or because she has just been busy studying the world from this new and interesting perspective. Discovering that sitting actually gives you more, rather than less, freedom is an important step that pushes the infant to develop the strength and balance to sit alone. So, by four months, although she still relies completely on your help to get into the sitting position, she now really begins to apply her own strength to maintain it. For some infants, an intermediate solution is to prop themselves up by leaning forwards on to their hands.

As long as the baby is first placed in the seated position, at around five months her muscles are strong enough for her to maintain her balance unaided, although only momentarily at this stage. Several weeks of practice later, she is ready to lever herself into the position by holding on to your hands and pulling her body weight up. At six months, however, she can still only remain seated alone for about thirty seconds before losing her balance and toppling over. The drive to sit is nevertheless relentless, and the frustration of finding herself lying flat again only spurs her on to try once more. She will still turn to you for assistance, though she is increasingly using her own strength to push herself up. Soon she will discover that she can also substitute your helping hands for your trouser legs, pieces of furniture or the bars of her cot to hoist herself into a seated position. So, by about seven or eight months, your baby has become quite a proficient sitter, and learns to coordinate a whole range of other movements such as twisting the upper body, reaching and pointing while maintaining this stable posture.

One of the trickiest things babies have to learn in relation to sitting is to find the correct centre of gravity to keep their upper body upright. Establishing and maintaining balance is a difficult puzzle. It involves steadying the waist area and using the hips and bottom as a base. The centre of gravity must start right in the middle of this base and be maintained all the way up the spine and to the top of the head. There is a lot of room for error here. A tiny

'Look, no hands.' This baby's happy confidence in his ability to sit unaided was a bit premature – as he discovered a moment later!

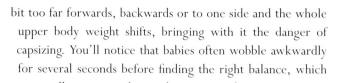

bit too far forwards, backwards or to one side and the whole upper body weight shifts, bringing with it the danger of capsizing. You'll notice that babies often wobble awkwardly for several seconds before finding the right balance, which usually goes together with an amusingly serious expression of deep concentration. Different babies discover different ways of solving this problem. Some adopt a lotus position, using their legs and feet bent in towards the body to steady their weight slightly forwards. Others prefer to sit with their legs wide apart. Both positions increase the size of the sitting base, and are good ways of preventing toppling over, as the legs can be used to counterbalance any shifts in body weight.

Sitting up is an important developmental milestone, not only in terms of motor coordination and control, but also in terms of intellectual development. The baby's visual range when lying down is far more restricted than it is when she's upright. On her back, she can look at the ceiling, and to the sides as far as the mattress will allow — but there isn't always much to look at in the air. Now that she can sit unsupported, she is in a much better position to scan the room. She can turn her head and twist her trunk round to extend her field of vision significantly without restriction from the supports she needed previously. Above all, her hands are now free to explore the things around her. Toys that were once out of reach can now be stretched to by relying not only on the actual length of her arm and hand, but by bending and extending the upper body towards the desired goal.

How do I get from A to B?

I've invented a way of moving from one place to another on all fours. I was sure I was human, so why do I walk more like our dog than like my brother?

What you're doing is not a special form of 'walking', but crawling. You have just learned that you're now strong enough to raise your upper body off the floor, and this allows you to use your legs and arms to propel yourself forwards or backwards. This is an important development as you are now really on the move for the first time.

CRAWLING   This may seem simple enough — something we adults could do, if necessary, without thinking. But can you describe the series of movements that make up a crawl without actually getting down on the floor and trying it out? Think about it for a minute: how does your baby crawl? These same questions were put to parents in one experiment, and the outcome was rather amusing. The adults gave all sorts of different accounts, the most common being that babies first move one hand forwards followed by the other, and then bring the legs forwards one at a time. If this were indeed the case, the infant would progress at a snail's pace, and might eventually overextend her arms to pick up speed, only to find herself flattened on the floor! An alternative description was that babies move their left arm and left leg simultaneously, followed by the right arm and right leg. This would certainly accelerate things, but if you tried it yourself you would discover just how hard it is to maintain your balance with your body weight shifting completely from one side to the other at every move. In many cases, adults finally had to resort to getting down on to the floor themselves before they could describe correctly the complex pattern of movements involved in a baby's crawl.

For a long time, scientists believed that crawling involved moving one limb at a time while balancing the centre of gravity over a tripod-shape created by the other three. In fact, careful observation using transparent surfaces over which infants were made to crawl revealed that there is a universal pattern of interlimb coordination involved in hands-and-knees crawling. Babies who crawl on all fours alternate between the two pairs of diagonal limbs. So, baby first moves one pair (left hand with right knee), then the other (right hand with left knee). This is called a 'dynamic balance system' and is actually the most efficient way of moving forwards on all fours. The centre of gravity is maintained around one small area at each movement, and the sequence is quick and easy to alternate.

Amazingly, this crawling action is so reliable and stable that it is not affected by adding weights to the baby's body, or by increasing the incline of the surface on which the baby is crawling. Experiments have shown that with a lot of practice, babies can crawl up surfaces sloping as much as 70 degrees.

Although crawling movements can be seen as early as two weeks, when babies manage to creep up their blankets (*page 113*), these actions are involuntary. They are not constructed along any particular patterns of movements; nor are they a means of locomotion in the way that crawling is. Even belly crawling, or creeping, which some babies adopt at around 32 weeks, is not characterised by a well-coordinated pattern of movements, but rather involves combining pulling, pushing and shuffling of the body using the legs and bent arms to produce movement. It may be fairly successful, but it is a clumsy way of getting from A to B and not at all energy efficient. Minimising the amount of energy needed to produce movement is the primary objective of adopting

In the early stages of learning to crawl, it is easy to get the sequence of movements slightly wrong. This baby has moved her arms too far forwards and is now balanced in this rather precarious position. One movement more and she'll be flat on her stomach!

HOW CRAWLING STRUCTURES THE BRAIN

Research has shown that during infancy, crawling experience modifies some aspects of the brain's organisation in parts of the cortex. One study examined brain processes in four groups of eight-month-old infants with differing hands-and-knees crawling experience. Group 1 was not yet able to crawl at all; Group 2 were novice crawlers with between one and four weeks of experience; Group 3 had five to eight weeks' experience of crawling; and Group 4 were long-term crawlers with more than two months of experience. When groups of cells (neurons) fire in different parts of the cortex, electrical activity is produced and brain waves can be measured by a technique known as electroencephalography (EEG). Recordings were taken from several cortical regions of the infants' left and the right hemispheres. Scientists calculated whether the timing of brain waves in different regions in the two hemispheres was related and found significant differences between the groups of infants. Group 2 showed more coherent time-related brain waves across the two hemispheres than either the pre-crawlers of Group 1 or the two groups of more experienced crawlers. This suggests that the anticipation and onset of locomotion is related to an initial overproduction of connections between different cortical regions. As crawling becomes more automatised and routine, connections between different cortical areas are pruned back and less of the brain fires when crawling. This is probably because, once the infant is an expert crawler, the brain no longer requires as much involvement from the occipital cortex (used for visual processing as the child moves forwards), the parietal cortex (where complex integration of the different senses takes place), nor the frontal cortex (used for conscious planning and prediction). In other words, just prior to starting to crawl, the infant brain prepares itself by overproducing connections between neurons in different parts of the cortex, but as crawling becomes increasingly efficient, only the essential connections are strengthened and retained.

a particular means of locomotion. This is true not only for humans but for most species. While other animals tend to use more energy for moving around than for any other activity, human beings (whose energy is conserved in particular for the activities of the evolving brain) select the method of mobility at each stage of motor development that is the least costly in terms of energy required. Thus, when very young, infants do not really move at all. Their bodies are not mature enough to produce energy-saving movement so they stay put. With time, however, their muscles grow strong enough to support the abdomen off the ground and they find themselves on all fours. They can now move forwards without an overwhelming amount of effort.

Hands-and-knees crawling, which emerges some time around 42 weeks, indicates that, upon reaching a certain stage in muscle control and development, the baby has selected the most efficient pattern of movement. Though it sounds like an incredibly clever feat, actually this often happens by mistake. A baby sitting and playing happily will drop her toy, reach forwards to retrieve it, and in tilting over, find herself on all fours. She will then test the potential of this position by rocking, reaching, lifting an arm or a leg, until she discovers that the right combination produces exciting movement. Amusingly, this movement sometimes drives the baby backwards! Many parents are astonished to find that their child is a most proficient backwards-crawler, but seems incapable of going forwards. This is because at this stage the muscles in the arms are stronger than those in the legs, and may propel the baby in the wrong direction. The problem is that once she discovers that a certain posture and series of movements can make her mobile, she will endeavour to reproduce them as often as possible. If this happens to put her into reverse gear at first, it may take another chance discovery ('I can go in the opposite direction if I push harder against my legs') to propel her forwards.

Not all babies crawl. Some save themselves for the even more energy-efficient means of locomotion – bipedal walking. They go straight from sitting to cruising (*see pages 126–7*). Those that never adopt hands-and-knees crawling (about twelve to eighteen per cent of babies), may find other solutions to the problem of getting from A to B before they are ready to stand and walk. They may bottom shuffle, for instance, or bear- or spider-walk (with hands and feet on the floor, bottom in the air). This can result in surprisingly speedy movement, though none of these alternatives can match regular crawling in terms of efficiency, stability and versatility.

Somewhat inelegant, perhaps, but bear- or spider-walking is a pretty fast way of moving around.

Crawling gives the baby a new sense of freedom – freedom to properly explore her environment. Like sitting, it isn't just a milestone for motor development, but also a real step forwards intellectually. As she crosses the room one way, she builds up a picture or map of her surroundings, but when it's time to return to her starting point, she realises that she can choose a number of alternative routes back and create alternative maps. Spatial coordination and understanding develop significantly as a result of the onset of crawling. And this, in turn, means the emergence of new knowledge about depth, distance, the properties of different surfaces (slippery, rough, smooth, sticky) and the dangers that may lurk around the corner.

Wow! I've just managed to pull myself up on to my two feet by using the bars of my cot. I like it up here. Is this just a one-off, or have I seen the last of life on all fours?

Not quite, this is only the beginning of your life as a biped. You're still going to need to get back down on to the floor in order to actually move! It'll take lots of practice and quite a bit of falling over before you feel confident enough to abandon crawling altogether. At this stage, you're just getting to grips with standing up. You need to spend some time working out how to keep your balance on two limbs before you can stay upright and move at the same time.

Even at the young age of four months, babies like to practise standing when they're well supported. Bouncing up and down in this position helps to strengthen the leg and back muscles.

STANDING UP At around six or seven months, babies begin to practise standing from the sitting position if they are held tightly under the arms and can rely on your support. They flex their knees and bounce up on to their feet and down on to their bottoms. You will notice this particularly when you are holding your baby on your lap. From the big smile on her face, it's obviously great fun! But these little workouts actually play an important role in helping her develop her leg muscles and establish her balance in preparation for standing by herself. By approximately eight and a half months, she may begin to use your knees, trousers or handy pieces of furniture to haul herself into a standing position. She has discovered that her legs are strong enough to push her up and hold her body weight.

At around nine months, a baby's legs are still only about a third of her body length. If you compare this to your legs (which account for about half of your height), you can begin to understand why babies find standing so difficult at first. Their two little legs have to support two-thirds of their total body length, and this requires a lot of muscular power, coordination and mental determination. In fact, the initial difficulty for the baby who suddenly feels a strong urge to stand up is not so much how to get *up*, but rather how to get back *down* into the seated position. Changing the centre of gravity from sitting to standing takes place gradually and is much more controllable than vice versa. Picture yourself in slow motion going from a standing to a seated position. First you have to shift your balance forwards and stick out your bottom, while at the same time bending your knees and lowering your body. If you miss out one of these actions, you lose your balance and end up with a sore bottom! For the baby, this requires long sessions of practice, tentatively trying out different ways of reaching the floor again once she has stood up. She may try bending her knees up and down without letting go of her support, to see if she can safely lower her body far enough. Or she may opt for attempting a landing on all fours by letting herself fall gently forwards. Alternatively, she may just stand in her cot or hang on to the side of the sofa looking despondent or even cry until she is rescued, however long it takes. Most often, the standing game will finish with a crash-landing on the backside. This is when nappies really come in handy as padding for a soft landing!

This little boy clutches firmly on to his father's trouser leg to prevent him from wobbling too much as he struggles to his feet.

Many mammals are able to pull themselves up on to two limbs (their back legs), but they usually have to come back down on to three or four limbs in order to move. In contrast, the standing position is the beginning of the locomotion the human infant has been designed for. Although babies do not give up crawling for quite some time yet, the drive to walk on two legs is very strong once they have discovered how to stand up. They will adopt this position in as many different situations as possible, so long as it is safe to do so. Standing up opens a whole range of new opportunities for the child, such as climbing on to seats and sofas, discovering and reaching for things that were previously kept at a safe distance, way above her head. For several months, however, she will not attempt to stand unsupported for more than a brief moment. She can sense that her weight is not quite stable on her tiny legs. Finally, by about eleven months she will begin to stand alone without holding on to something, but it isn't until she is a proficient toddler, at around two and a half, that she will be completely secure and stable on her feet.

At last, I'm on the move on two feet. But I fall over if I don't hold on to things. It's a slower way of moving than crawling, and I get stuck whenever I reach a gap. Am I wasting my time moving around like this?

No, quite the contrary. What you are doing is called 'cruising', and it's a way of learning how to take single steps in order to get from one place to another. It's slow because you have to move each hand and foot one at a time while you hold on to something for support. But it is very good practice for walking. While crawling is fast and a lot less trouble, you can sense that your crawling days are almost over. You have a strong drive to get the hang of walking.

CRUISING Once your baby is stable in a standing position, cruising is just around the corner. It's a very natural progression which, although it does require a surprising amount of extra coordination and muscle-power, is still some way from proper bipedal walking. Even if assisted by an adult's steadying hand, walking relies primarily on being able to transfer the body weight smoothly from one leg to the other. This is incredibly difficult to achieve. Cruising, on the other hand, makes use not only of the strength and control of the legs, but also of the power of the arms to pull and the chest and sides of the body to rest against a support, so that when one limb moves, the baby can retain her balance using various other parts of the body. With time, and growing cruising expertise, the infant reduces the number of body parts she uses to keep herself upright. Eventually, her hands are not really holding up her weight; they are merely used to guide each step.

Cruising is very much a halfway house in the infant's drive for locomotion. Less efficient than either crawling or walking in terms of time and effort, it emerges not so much as a replacement for previous forms of locomotion but rather as a learning process bridging the tricky gap separating crawling and walking skills. That said, not all babies go through a cruising phase, preferring to face the daunting challenge of walking unsupported once they have learned to stand unaided. Those who do choose to cruise generally begin doing so some time after nine months.

Cruising usually involves moving sideways along the length of a piece of furniture or a wall, much like a crab. As it relies on the hands as much as the feet, it is almost like a vertical form of crawling. But, as a means of getting about, it has serious limitations

'Mind the gap.' Cruising along the furniture can be challenging, particularly when the props inconveniently run out. This toddler resorts to crawling when she reaches a gap, but up she comes on two feet again once there's something to hold on to.

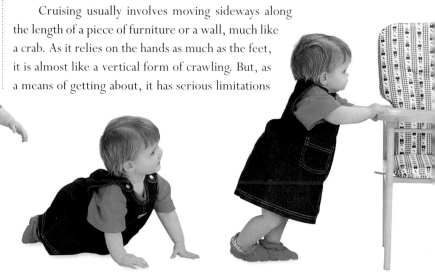

that hands-and-knees crawling does not. For instance, cruising consists of moving one limb at a time whereas, as we have seen, crawling involves an optimal pattern of movement using diagonal pairs of limbs (*see page 121*). Furthermore, while the support from furniture can run out, the floor surface generally does not. When cruising, the infant is faced with a real dilemma about how to get across gaps between objects to cling on to. This is all good exercise for the brain, however. Babies will work through a number of options. For example, can I stretch my arm far enough to grab hold of the next piece of furniture? To answer that question she has to take into account distance relationships. She also discovers something about her own size in relation to other things. And, in attempting to reach over the gap, she finds out what happens if you propel your weight forwards and let go of your support. Many babies solve the problem by resorting to crawling or bottom-shuffling. But, interestingly, they will usually only make use of these established skills long enough to reach the next prop and begin cruising again.

It is thought that the drive to walk is partly caused by the limitations that both crawling and cruising place on the infant's use of her hands. It is very difficult and cumbersome to crawl or cruise while carrying a toy, for example. Furthermore, in order to point or reach for something, she would have to stop moving. This is obviously not the case for walking, which truly frees up the arms and hands while at the same time allowing the baby to reach her goal.

FIRST STEPS Parents never forget the first time they see their baby take her first steps. Although they are probably unaware of just how momentous an achievement these initial risky and wobbly steps are, seeing their little one on two legs and walking alone is still a real thrill. At that moment, their baby becomes a toddler and a whole new world opens up. The child senses her parents' enthusiasm, feels a real sense of having done something special, something rewarding, and strives to achieve this again. These memorable experiences also serve as important moments of bonding.

The road to bipedal walking is a long and complicated one, full of obstacles, puzzles for the baby to solve, and requiring plenty of patience, strength and determination. To fully understand why walking

You'd think I'd won an Olympic medal the way mum and dad are carrying on! All I did was let go of the sofa and take a few wobbly steps towards them. I didn't even make it across the carpet without falling on my bottom twice. Luckily I'm wearing nappies which cushion my fall. So why are my parents so excited?

You took your first steps alone today, and this is as exciting for your mum and dad as hearing your first words. They see it as the culmination of all your months of effort in learning to sit, crawl and then stand by yourself. Being able to walk is a real breakthrough, and makes you appear a lot more grown up and independent than before.

Almost a walker, this little boy is doing all he can to keep erect: legs splayed and arms out in anticipation of a fall. A few more days of practice and he'll be a biped.

takes quite so long to emerge, we have to go back in time. As we saw in the chapter on Being Born, one of the most noticeable reflexes at birth is the stepping reflex whereby, when held upright with the feet touching a firm surface, the newborn automatically makes walking movements with her legs (*pages 39–40*). Although this action involves all the same body parts and muscular structure as proper unsupported bipedal walking, at this stage the infant is completely incapable of achieving balance or supporting her weight. All her muscles are in place, but they are weak and undeveloped, and the steps she takes are involuntary reflex actions over which she has no control. However, scientists have shown that the newborn's leg movements, even on her back, are important for the building of muscles, which explains why very young babies spend so much time vigorously working out by kicking their legs.

From around eight weeks, most babies give up 'walking' when held upright, instead letting their legs dangle limply. It is thought that as infants grow and lay down fat, their legs become too heavy to lift when upright (bending and straightening the legs from a horizontal posture is much easier, which is why babies practise their kicking when they are lying down, sitting, being held or in the bath). Gravity is therefore the main culprit in bringing about the demise of the walking reflex. This has been confirmed by experiments in which newborns had little weights attached to their legs. The extra weight caused a dramatic reduction in the walking reflex. Similarly, an increase in the frequency and vigour of the reflex was found in older infants when they were submerged up to the torso in water, surmounting the gravity problem. But this is not the end of the story. Experience can also play a role in the development of certain motor behaviours, including the walking reflex. Studies have shown that in cultures where walking is highly valued and actively encouraged from birth, the stepping reflex tends not to disappear at two months, but continues until the emergence of unsupported walking at the end of the first year. Babies in communities such as the Kipsigis tribe from Kenya are given a lot of regular stepping practice throughout infancy, and are actively pushed to concentrate on this skill. It is likely that these babies develop their leg muscles more quickly, and this results in a slightly earlier onset of unsupported walking. On average, Kipsigis babies start walking about one month earlier than Western infants. However, there is no real long-term advantage in speeding up motor development in this way. Data show that these early walkers were in fact behind in mastering those skills less highly valued by their cultures, such as early head control and crawling. So practice in one skill has only very local effects and does not speed up other forms of motor control.

The age at which babies take their first tentative steps varies dramatically between individuals. Some infants may bravely step out unsupported as early as eleven months, while others prefer to play it safe and wait until they are fifteen or twenty months. Whatever the age, babies need to take their time to develop enough confidence, balance and strength before they feel ready to take off alone. This is because the walking business is much more complex and difficult to achieve than one might think. The challenge comes from having to do two different things with each leg: stabilise the body on one of the legs while simultaneously thrusting forwards with the other. In taking a step, we actually have to push the ground away with one leg, in the opposite direction (backwards) to the one in which we are actually heading (forwards). This all has to be done with the correct amount of force so we

This little fellow is taking his first steps into mum's welcoming open arms.

don't lose our balance as our centre of gravity is transferred smoothly from one foot to the other to complete the step. However, we do actually create a momentary imbalance: at the point when our centre of mass has been propelled ahead of one leg, the other leg is being swung forwards to support the body and move us on. In order to walk, this whole process must then be reiterated over and over again. Faced with such a complicated task at each step, it isn't surprising that the human infant requires long months of preparation before she is ready to begin walking bipedally.

To overcome the difficulties of walking, babies often adopt various clever, though amusing-looking, strategies. Some may hold their arms out to each side, high above their heads, as a counterbalance. Others will initially walk with their legs spread wide apart and feet turned out, waddling from one leg to the other like little ducks. However, having cracked this difficult challenge, they take every opportunity to practise, and soon become more proficient and confident walkers, able to make quite a smooth transition between walking and sitting, and even managing to drag a toy behind them as they walk.

LOOKING AHEAD **Some time around your baby's second birthday, she will begin to refine her walking skills, learning how to stop, change direction, accelerate and decelerate without landing on her bottom each time. As her muscles strengthen and her body gradually elongates over the months, her steps will become less precarious, her balance will improve and she will slowly leave behind the wobbly gait of the fledgling walker. Soon she will be hopping, skipping, jumping and dancing with true confidence.**

Now I'm a bit steadier on my feet, I'd like to be able to go up and down stairs, run and skip, hop and jump, dance and kick like a football player. When will I be able to keep up with my brother and sister's movement?

Although you've now acquired much of the motor coordination and control you need, you're still quite a long way from knowing all there is to know about movement. You spent two long years striving to develop the ability to get from A to B without help, and now you're able to concentrate on learning lots of new and interesting tricks using your motor skills.

THE FULLY FLEDGED BIPED Well before they are competent walkers, toddlers may start stair climbing. This usually takes place about six months after the onset of walking. Climbing up is much easier than climbing down, however, so you may find your child stuck halfway up the stairs, unable to work out how to descend. Initially, toddlers use a mixture of crawling and walking to go up stairs. They don't climb with alternate feet; rather, they move up a step at a time, using one knee to lead the way and support the body as the opposite leg is brought up. They then start the whole process again for the next step. Later they may climb without coming down on one knee, but still bring both feet to rest on each stair. However, at this stage, babies can use their skills to go one way only – climbing down again is achieved on their bottoms! It isn't until about 25 months that toddlers master the art of walking down stairs one step at a time. And only at roughly 30 months have they perfected their stair-climbing skills and developed enough confidence to climb alternate steps in both directions.

By the end of the second year of life, most toddlers are competent walkers, their gait almost resembling that of an adult. Their legs are fairly close together, toes facing forwards, and their arms swing from side to side close to their body. But locomotor skills don't transcend merely to walking. There are numerous other abilities that bipedalism makes possible.

Two to six months after those first unsteady steps, the infant may try combining her steps in an increasingly fast cycle to produce what eventually looks like running. But the running action is significantly different from the walking movement and this makes it difficult to master at first. For instance, whereas a walk is made up of a series of well-coordinated footfalls, running involves a series of well-controlled leaps. The running movement has what is called a 'flight phase' during which neither foot is in contact with the ground. It is thought that improved coordination alone is not sufficient to allow the child to make the transition from walking to running. Instead, scientists believe that changing body proportions and the ability to send rapid messages from the brain to the muscles creates the force and motor control necessary to run.

About six months after they start running, toddlers master a series of other movements including galloping, hopping, jumping and kicking, and finally may combine all these abilities when you turn on some lively music to produce their own little dances. These skills involve not only intricate patterns of interlimb coordination, but also different activities in the brain. The development of a whole range of motor skills may go unnoticed by parents once their baby has learned to walk. But being attentive to such changes can be rewarding, as each new ability indicates a step forwards in your child's life.

Running, dancing, hopping: nothing will hold this young biped back now.

Learning to Use My Hands

When you picked up this book and turned the pages, you probably saw nothing remarkable in your actions. But stop for a moment and think about how perfectly you (or, rather, your brain) prepared your hand shape for the size, shape and texture of the book, and how your thumb and index finger were delicately coordinated to take hold of each page. It will be a long time before your infant's hands can do anything that intricate. But there's still a particularly special thrill about the moments when he first reaches for and grasps his mobile, or bangs a spoon on his cot to make 'music' or, later, when he finally manages to pick up a tiny raisin by pinching together his index finger and thumb. Developments in object manipulation are quite noticeable and go hand-in-hand with advances in your infant's independence. Once he learns to take hold of objects, he no longer has to wait for the world to be brought to him. He can choose which toys to play with, and can also make them move and come into contact with one another. He is increasingly in control of his ever-expanding environment.

The sites in the brain responsible for motor coordination need to become intricately tied up with other parts of the brain in order for these advances to take place. So, for instance, it is at the time when infants' hand-to-eye coordination is developing the most rapidly, at around three to four months of age, that a sudden burst of synaptic activity is triggered in the visual cortex. By contrast, the prefrontal cortex *(the part of the brain responsible, inter alia, for planning fine movement) is on a different developmental timetable: although it begins forming connections at birth, increases in synaptogenesis are much slower for this part of the brain, which is why manual dexterity takes much longer to emerge than the more primitive hand-to-eye coordination. While this process requires some time, the more your infant manipulates objects of different shapes and sizes, the more he will strengthen the developing pathways in the brain for fine motor control. So experience is also important and parents can certainly help their child's development in this domain. For example, you could give your baby a series of objects differing in shape and size, so that he constantly has*

to change the shape of his grasp. If you could watch the activity in his brain as he prepares to take each new object, you would see how the object's particular properties cause different pathways to be activated.

· ·

Fine motor control is crucial to an infant's overall intellectual development. Research has shown that measures of fine motor dexterity in eighteen-month-olds can actually predict what level of language acquisition and cognitive development will be achieved at the age of six. This is because motor aptitude involves far more than mere handling skills. It is intricately linked to overall intellectual development. Complex, dynamic interactions across the brain connect motor circuits to the child's visual system, as well as to the prefrontal cortex. This allows the brain to anticipate and plan how the hand should be prepared as the baby reaches either for a large, soft teddy bear next to him or for a hard, narrow pencil on the shelf. In other words, the brain calculates the size, texture and distance of an object each time the child reaches for something. This activity in the brain then produces complex sequences of actions needed to handle a whole range of objects.

While object manipulation opens up a whole new world of entertainment for the baby, one of the most crucial aspects of manual dexterity is that it allows us to use tools in ways that no other species can. Take a pen or pencil and write a couple of words, then draw a face with eyes, nose, a mouth, ears and a beard. It's automatic. Now do it again, but this time watch your hand carefully and marvel at the complexity of control that allows you to write and draw. First, notice how different it feels to write a word as opposed to make a sketch. Then think about the very different movements of your pen when you direct it to drawing the eyes compared to the squiggles of the beard. It will be some time before your infant will even be able to hold a pen, let alone be capable of making small straight or circular movements to leave a trace on the paper. But when he does, he will be en route to becoming a fully fledged tool user. Once your child can manipulate tools, his capacity to control his world takes on new dimensions. Objects like a lever can increase his ability to move things, a stick can extend his reach and a key can open new doors. Finally, he can learn to feed and dress himself and thereby gain even more independence.

How do I grab hold of that toy?

I have this habit of taking a swing at things I see in front of me. I don't seem to achieve much, though. So what are these strange arm exercises all about?

What you're doing is a form of pre-reaching. Your hand-to-eye coordination is still immature so you're not yet in a position to reach out and grab things. Swiping – which is what you have been doing – is your way of bringing your arm into contact with something you find interesting and at arm's reach. It may seem clumsy, but it's quite an achievement and very good practice for developing better control over your arm and hand movements.

SWIPING Some of the earliest visible manifestations of goal-oriented behaviour in the infant are movements such as swiping and, later, proper reaching. While such actions may seem incredibly rudimentary, they in fact indicate that the baby is successfully combining and integrating information from different parts of the brain in order to accomplish his goal. In the case of swiping, motor control of the arm is matched with visual information about the distance of the object from the baby. Unlike later reaching and grasping, which involve finer control of all the muscles in the arm, wrist, hand and fingers, the swiping action comprises fairly crude muscular activity of the shoulder and elbow, the aim of which is to bring the limb into contact with an object he has been looking at. Contact is the first step.

Right from birth, the infant makes swiping movements with his arms, but at first these are not directed at anything. They are involuntary reflex movements designed to increase arm strength. After a few weeks, however, he

Enhancing early muscular control

Stimulating your young baby to use his muscles and improve his coordination can help him develop control over his movements. Swiping is very good practice for reaching and grasping, and can be encouraged during the first two months. Hang an interesting mobile just above the changing table, low enough for your baby's arm to reach up and just touch it. When he is lying on his back, calm and alert, attract his attention to the mobile and to the way it moves. He may fixate on it for a moment, and then he will extend his arm excitedly towards it. If he does not make

contact, move the mobile slightly so it touches his hand, thereby showing him that his own actions can have interesting results. If he does not make any effort to reach from this position, try picking him up and while he is in an upright position, hold a toy such as a rattle a few inches away from him. Posture and gravity play significant roles in complicating or facilitating motor control, especially at an early age, so your infant may find it easier to swipe outwards rather than up. Again, attract his attention to the rattle by talking to him and wiggling the toy. Babies as young as three weeks attempt to swipe at objects, and this can be fun for both of you.

starts to gain better control over the muscles of his limbs, and you may begin to notice that he is intentionally stretching his arms out in the direction of things that have captivated his attention. Fascinatingly, he will generally do so only if the target object is within reach of his little arm, suggesting that he already perceives vital information about how far away the object is and where it is in relation to other objects nearby.

As we have seen, motor development progresses not only from head to toe, but also from the centre of the body outwards – that is, from coarse and general control of the limbs to increasingly fine control of limb parts and extremities (*see page 110*). Thus, the baby is able intentionally to move his arm as a whole some time before he can master wrist, hand and finger action. It is also known that the pathways in the brain responsible for perceiving and locating things in the environ-ment develop earlier than the pathways responsible for voluntary action. So, while the newborn is adept at locating a sound or light, for instance, he has difficulty controlling his actions to track the noise or light smoothly by moving his eyes and head. Similarly, when a young baby sees a toy suspended within tantalising reach, he may be able to perceive its location in relation to himself quite expertly, but if he tries to touch it, his planned movement is fairly crude and he can only wave his arm in its general direction – or, if he's lucky, perhaps hit it with his clenched fist.

Although these simple movements may seem a rather crude and unpro-ductive endeavour, swiping actually plays an important role in promoting improved motor control and intellectual development. Lying on the changing table or in the cot watching the mobile dancing above him, the baby sets himself a problem: how do I find out more about this interesting thing? He formulates the goal of touching the mobile, and executes it by lifting his arm and swiping in the direction of the mobile. If all goes to plan, his action causes him first to make contact with the object, which then moves or perhaps even makes a sound. As a result, his brain makes new connections about the outcomes of his behaviour and he is spurred on to try out further attempts. Within a few weeks, his fingers gradually uncurl and he is able to swipe with open hands. This helps him aim better, increases contact with the target and results in making the mobile move in all sorts of new and interesting ways. And the cycle begins again, with further attempts to swipe in different ways and new discoveries about the whole range of outcomes which his actions cause. This is a period during which infants tend to show increasing interest in the objects around them.

An attractive mobile provides the perfect practice for swiping. This little six-week-old has actually managed to make contact with the toy.

I'm getting much better at using my arms. I've discovered that I don't need to look at my hands before I stretch my arm out for something. I can even find objects when I reach for them in the dark. So how do my arms know where to go?

Your arms are responding to special messages from your brain. Even without looking down at your hands, you're able to perceive the location of an object and form a map which your brain then uses to guide your arm movements. At first, your reaching action is not as straight as an adult's, but with experience you'll become more and more adept at it.

LEARNING TO REACH The change from swiping to a much more controlled form of reaching occurs as a result of weeks of practice involving trial and error. With experience, the baby is able to form memories of which arm movements were successful and which were not. Success motivates him to reproduce the same arm movements in different situations, so he gradually becomes increasingly accurate at reaching for objects which he perceives as within reach. His body posture will still place constraints on his efforts to use his arms and hands, however. For example, babies who are not yet able to sit unsupported have difficulty reaching with one arm if they are propped up in this position. They generally opt for a two-handed reach, or even use their feet to lead the reaching action and make contact with the object. This is because their efforts are divided between staying well supported and balanced while at the same time stretching out to the target. This also means that they cannot lean forwards in order to extend their reach. All these limitations disappear once babies achieve unsupported sitting, enabling the infant to reach with increasing accuracy and flexibility.

Studies have found interesting differences between the way infants and adults reach for things. By carefully mapping the movements of the baby's arm when he is reaching out, scientists have been able to compare the patterns of infant arm control with those of a grown-up. It transpires that the adult's arm makes a single, large, bell-shaped movement when reaching for something, whereas the baby's reach is made up of a series of movement units, or sub-movements. At around four months of age, when babies begin to reach rather than swipe, a single reaching action towards a desired toy might consist of up to five separate sub-movements. This is not to say that he makes five separate attempts before getting it right. He is much cleverer and more coordinated than that! Rather, he has worked out the best strategy to employ within his limited abilities. At such a young age, he still has difficulty predicting the exact outcome of a single motor command to his arm. It is therefore safer to opt for several smaller arm movements, each of which can be slightly adjusted if it is off course, rather than a single sweeping action which may send the arm further off its planned trajectory. There is one interesting exception to this rule. If the baby intends only to hit the target object, he will take the chance on a single, large arm movement, probably because it requires far less precision than reaching out to actually grasp a toy.

By about five months, babies have gained extensive knowledge of spatial relationships between objects and have acquired good eye, arm and hand coordination. This allows them to accomplish very accurate reaching in all sorts of different situations. When babies reach out to an object, it is important not to confuse this with pointing, which develops at about six months. Babies will point (with a different hand shape to reaching) at distant objects that interest them, but they do not intentionally stretch out to grasp objects out of reach. They already know quite a lot about distances between themselves and objects and understand that such efforts would be a waste of time.

At eight or nine months, infants are even able to reach accurately in the dark towards objects that make a noise, like a rattle, which they realise are within reach. What's more, by this stage they begin anticipating the size and shape of the object they are reaching for, even if it is concealed from sight. So, if they reach in the dark for an object that sounds big (a deep-sounding gong, say), they will do so with both arms and the fingers stretched out wide. Conversely, if the object sounds small (the high-pitched ring of a small bell), they will choose a single-handed reach with the thumb opposing the fingers to increase grasping control. The ability to grasp successfully an object under these conditions is quite remarkable when you consider that the infant cannot use his sense of vision to guide his hands.

A further amazing ability infants display during the second half of the first year is to reach for moving objects. This is a skill we take for granted, but it actually involves not only excellent coordination, but also careful planning. To grab a ball swinging at the end of string in front of him, the baby must anticipate its speed and trajectory in order to decide how best to intercept it. Initially, this may prove too difficult, and many attempts result in failure. Undeterred, however, the infant will persist until he finds the best strategy. If the ball is moving from his right to his left, instead of choosing to reach with the right hand, which was initially nearest to the ball, he discovers the importance of anticipation, that reaching with the left hand gives him more time to move before the toy disappears out of reach again. Thus, what seem at first to be simple motor actions turn out to be impressively complex intellectual acts, involving being able to judge distance, speed and size, and the planning of a series of interrelated actions.

This six-month-old is so intent on using both hands to grasp the enticing toy being held just beyond his reach that he is in danger of toppling over.

These hands of mine are great! They used to have a mind of their own, and remained either curled up or splayed out, but now I've started being able to stretch them out and touch things. Will I at last be able to hold on to the toys I reach for?

From now on you'll become increasingly good at picking up and manipulating objects with your hands. When you were born, you had little control over the muscles of your hands. But as you become stronger and more coordinated, little messages are sent to your brain to make your hands and fingers execute intentional and increasingly diverse movements.

GRASPING Reaching is intimately bound up with the development of grasping and exploring objects. Babies are born with a strong grasping reflex whereby their little fingers close tightly around any object that comes into contact with the centre of their palms (*see also pages 38–9*). These automatic movements play a role in activating and building up the muscles of the hand. But they are merely reflexes, not purposeful, and they begin to disappear as the infant gains increasingly fine motor control.

The grasping reflex is very different from intentional grasping, which emerges sometime between two and four months. By this age, babies deliberately grip things pressed into their hand. But at first they do so rather primitively, using the thumb as one of the fingers, opening the hand as wide as possible before closing it around the object. The object is held against the half of the palm furthest from the thumb, which allows very limited manipulation control. At this young age, babies fail to take into account the size and shape of the object, and may have difficulty with small or strangely shaped objects. Young babies also find it very difficult to *let go* voluntarily, as mums with long hair quickly discover! They often need to be distracted with another object if they are to lose interest in – and let go of – the first object and grasp the second. But by nine months, babies can

Stimulating reaching and grasping skills

There are many games you can play with your baby, from six months, that will give you an idea of the progress he is making in his manual skills. Hold an attractive toy within reaching distance of your baby and slightly to the right. Let him get it a few times. Then, as he goes to reach for the object again, move it slowly towards the other side so he has to correct his reach. Be sure to make the game fun for your baby and adopt a very encouraging tone of voice. Alternatively, you could take two objects from the kitchen, one very small like a spoon, and the other considerably larger, like a mug. Hand them to your baby one after the other, and watch whether his hands start to adapt their shape in anticipation of the size of each object. Again, talk him

through the game, laughing and praising his efforts. Change the size of the objects every four or five turns – hand him an even larger object, a plastic mixing bowl, for example – and see how he now moves both his hands up to grasp it. Also, try giving him a selection of unbreakable utensils (plastic cups, spoons, trays, wooden spatulas) and watch how he tries shaking, banging and pushing each of these objects in different ways. The period from six to twelve months is the perfect time to start introducing lots of interesting and varied toys that encourage the development of exploration. For example, objects covered in different textures encourage sensitivity to touch, while toys that emit a variety of sounds when squeezed will captivate your baby's imagination for hours.

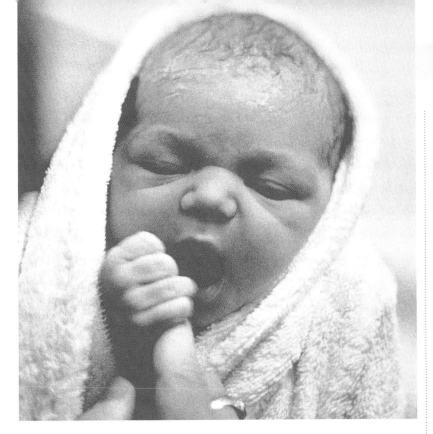

The grasping reflex has this newborn clutching tightly on to his father's finger. Yet at this age he shows no interest in what his hand is actually holding.

inhibit the grasping reflex completely. They are able to grip and let go easily, as well as to push away one toy without grasping it in their endeavour to take hold of the more appealing toy behind it.

Around three to four months, infants become interested in their feet and may bring their legs up to assist with holding an object when they are lying on their backs. This extra support enables them to use their flattened hands to pat the object in order to find out more about it. By around five months the baby begins to use his thumb in partial opposition to his fingers when grasping things, thus holding them more securely. This new development also means that he is able to pass an object from one hand to the other, and to let go of it by carefully loosening his grip. He now begins to shake the toys he picks up to see if they make interesting sounds. Then, from six months onwards, he increasingly uses his hands not only to grasp objects, but also to explore their properties. He fingers and palpates each toy to find out how hard or squashy, large or heavy it is, what shape it is, and whether he can create any sounds by banging it against a surface. He may also explore the surface of the toy, especially if it has a variety of different textures, and will learn that solid objects are graspable, whereas liquids and soap bubbles are not. So grasping at things leads to important discoveries about the different properties of objects.

From six months onwards, the increasing use of exploratory manipulation, as opposed to simple voluntary grasping, marks an important development in hand–eye coordination. The infant starts making assumptions about

This eight-month-old has gone beyond simple grasping and now adjusts her hand to the shape and size of different objects.

the specific characteristics of the objects he sees, and can to some degree anticipate their size, shape and texture even before touching them. As he reaches for a toy, he will shape his hand appropriately. Objects are now held against the portion of the hand nearest the index finger and thumb, which also allows for much more precise handling. Depending on the appearance of an object, the infant will adapt his grasp to handle it firmly or delicately. With their much-improved hand and finger control, six-month-old infants manipulate different objects in very different ways. For instance, they will scratch at a rough, sandy-looking ball, and listen for the interesting sound this makes. In contrast, they will stroke a furry surface. They will also squeeze a soft toy, while bumpy surfaces or those with holes in will be investigated with the tips of their fingers.

Grasping goes well beyond mere motor control. Through adapting to different kinds of objects, the brain builds up rich, interconnecting circuits within and between the cerebellum (important for muscle coordination, balance and the timing of action), the motor cortex which governs different types of action, and the frontal lobes responsible for planning and anticipatory action.

I've started collecting tiny things! There's the bead from mum's necklace, the button from dad's shirt and even a dead ant I found under the table. Why am I so interested in anything small?

You're suddenly fascinated with little objects because for the first time you have the ability to pick them up and inspect them properly. Up to now, you've been clumsily using all your fingers together, which meant you could only scoop up somewhat larger toys.

THE PINCER GRASP At around six months, babies begin attempting to pick up every small object that captures their attention. Although their hand-to-eye coordination is fairly well developed by this stage, control over very fine motor movements of the fingers and toes is still being perfected. Six-month-olds have yet to master finger-and-thumb grasping – known as the 'pincer grasp' or 'pincer grip' – and often try to scoop up little objects by pushing them with the side of one hand on to the open palm of the other. This is quite an ingenious solution to the limitations of their manual abilities, but it does not allow the child properly to inspect his catch. Having successfully scooped several beads into his hand, for instance, he remains unable to select the most colourful or preferred one for closer inspection, to roll it around in his palm or to bring it up to eye level with his fingers in order to see it from every angle. It isn't until about nine months of age, around the time when the baby is using his index fingers to point at things, that what is known as 'complete finger prehension' occurs, allowing him to develop a neat pincer grasp. Total finger prehension is the ability to control one finger at a time and to use the thumb to oppose that finger when grasping something. This is an exclusively human characteristic. Even our clever cousin, the chimpanzee, can at best use only the opposition between his thumb and the rest of his fingers all together to make a pinching hand shape.

The development of the pincer grasp is an important motor milestone because it provides the infant with dramatically increased precision when using his hands. No longer restricted by clumsy fingers, he won't waste any time putting his new skill into action. From the moment he discovers this new grip, the baby will turn his interest almost exclusively to little things just, it seems, for the sake of practising picking them up and putting them down again. It can be quite infuriating for a parent who has come home with an expensive, new, state-of-the-art baby toy only to find their child dismiss it within minutes in favour of concentrating on the ant making its way across the floor, or the button that just fell from your favourite shirt! Small items hold a new fascination simply due to their previously unattainable quality. But this type of play is not a fruitless pastime. Through hours of practice picking up little objects, the child develops increasing confidence in making very precise movements, and also learns to discriminate between small changes in objects' size, shape and weight.

Studies have shown that the development of the pincer grasp goes hand in hand with the growth of other more mature intellectual achievements. Babies start to be able to select the most appropriate grip for a given situation and to adapt their grasp to special circumstances. For example, experiments have indicated that babies of eight or nine months who normally have good finger-and-thumb abilities will resort to other, less mature ways of grasping if the small

The pincer grasp opens up a whole new world of tiny objects. This little girl has discovered the pleasure of feeding herself delicious tidbits such as raisins.

object (in this case a single Polo mint) to be picked up is on an unstable surface such as a wobbly tray. This is not the case a few months later. By thirteen to fourteen months of age, infants have worked out not only how to pluck something up easily, but also how to do so without disturbing the balance of the surface upon which the object rests, and will confidently pincer grasp the Polo mint from the tray.

The development of total finger prehension and the pincer grasp signals a time when parents should be extra cautious about what is left within their toddler's reach. Pills, beads and in fact anything small enough to be swallowed should be kept safely locked away. Plug sockets should be covered up as they may appear extremely inviting to the baby looking to bury his now mobile little fingers into all sorts of gaps. And when outside, watch out for unsuspecting little insects being plucked off the ground to be plunged into baby's open mouth! But this is also a positive period for your baby, as he can now take control of the activities you previously had to carry out. For instance, the pincer grasp allows him to turn the pages of a book, to control the rate at which a story is told and to linger on favourite pictures. This is also a time to develop threading hollow toys on to a shoe lace and the beginnings of buttoning and more successful self-feeding (*see pages 147–51*). If you want to help your infant develop his pincer grasp, you could give him raisins to eat or cut his apple into tiny pincer-grasp-sized pieces.

How do I control objects?

I've discovered a new trick! If I bang two toys together, it makes a great noise, or even better, they break up into lots of interesting bits. Mum and dad don't seem to share my enthusiasm for this game, though. Have I invented a special way to play, or am I just being destructive?

Although your parents may find it difficult to see your new game as creative, this is exactly what it is. You're comparing the properties of objects by bringing them together to see what noise they make and what effect the impact has on each toy. These little experiments are an important part of finding out about the world of physical things. Above all, right now they help you learn to coordinate both your hands simultaneously.

COORDINATING TWO OBJECTS The first time a baby brings two toys crashing together probably goes unnoticed by most parents, unless the two colliding objects happen to be pieces of your favourite china! To us, a child's new game may seem nothing more than novel way of making a loud noise. But for the infant it is an important step forwards. By coordinating two objects in this way, the child has made the crucial initial step towards tool use, by investigating for the first time how objects affect one another.

During the latter half of the first year, babies will spend a lot of their playtime manipulating all sorts of things: toys, objects left around the room, the edge of furniture, plants in the garden. As we have seen, in doing so they actively broaden their knowledge of the objects that fill their environment. Part of this process also involves discovering what happens when objects are brought together with force. Banging a xylophone with a wooden spoon, for instance, will produce a nice sound; a very different noise will be made using a metal spoon. Rapping teddy on the xylophone, in contrast, will not make much noise at all. All these discoveries are very interesting to the baby. Such activities are not simply about sound-production. Rather, the infant comes to understand that certain types of objects are made of material that resists impact, while others cave in, can be compressed slightly or squashed flat. This is an exciting discovery. The baby now finds that using a hard and rigid object to hit a ball sends the ball further than batting it with his soft, bendy fingers.

Having discovered how to bring one object into contact with a fixed, unmoving surface (such as the xylophone, the floor or a wall), the next step is to bring together two objects, one held in each hand. This is a far more difficult task, involving very different dynamics. The child has to learn to coordinate the movement in each of his arms and hands simultaneously. If the action is to result in the successful impact of the two toys, the trajectory of one hand has to be carefully matched to that of the other. But this doesn't simply involve good hand-to-eye coordination. The baby's posture plays a significant role too. Infants do not attempt to coordinate two objects until they can confidently sit unsupported, freeing not only their hands but also allowing well-controlled movement of the whole upper body.

Once he has discovered about impact, the baby will try other ways of coordinating the objects he is holding. He may attempt to fit one inside the other, attach one to the other, place them next to one another to compare their dimensions, or pile them up and then push them slightly to watch them topple. All these actions represent mini-lessons in physics. Construction toys or puzzles that encourage the child to fit certain shapes into different holes will now begin to have special appeal. You can also try giving your baby a set of different-sized plastic kitchen containers which fit neatly into each other, and watch how far he works out the correct order in which to place them.

This little girl's drumming (below left) may not be music to her parents' ears, but she is successfully coordinating two objects to produce sounds. Later, as manual dexterity develops further, babies begin to fit together the shapes of two objects in posting games, as this seventeen-month-old is doing (below right).

My favourite toys are inside that cupboard, and mum's busy talking to her friend. I'm not sure she'll hear if I cry for help, so how am I going to get them out by myself?

Instead of crying, showing frustration, and calling for help, you've now reached a stage when you can start using objects as tools, to give yourself extra abilities. So, in order to get the cupboard door open, you can try grabbing and turning the key sticking out of the lock. You've seen your parents do this, and while you're not yet sure what a key is or how it works, you know that it plays some role in getting the door to open. Tool use is an important skill about which you will continue to learn throughout your life.

LEARNING TO USE TOOLS It is important for you to be on the lookout for the onset of tool use, not only because it shows your baby at his most ingenious, but also because it may place him in dangerous situations as he gets increasingly inquisitive and creative with his use of objects. As babies become more familiar with the world of things, they begin to look for the hidden potential of objects. From twelve months onwards, they develop a new fascination for the buttons, switches, knobs and dials that stick out of machines, lights, taps and the like. At first, they may simply bang these interesting protrusions with their hands. Such early actions are more investigative than anything else, so infants may actually show considerable surprise when their behaviour results in turning the radio on or switching the light off. Very quickly, however, they formulate intelligent connections between actions and outcomes, and realise that in order to make one object do what they want it to do, they have to make use of another. The use of objects as tools now becomes a means to an end rather than simply an end in itself. This is very important, as the child discovers that by using tools he can greatly expand his ability to control his environment.

One of your baby's very first manifestations of tool use may be to use one object, such as a hairbrush, to reach another, such as a teddy bear sitting on a chair just out of reach. This involves clever planning and the understanding that one's reaching power is extended by holding, guiding and using a long object. The child must therefore be able to give the object a new, temporary and symbolic identity to fit that particular situation. So tool use is often closely related to developments in pretend play (*see pages 187–8*) and in the creation of ad hoc uses of objects: the hairbrush temporarily represents a stick.

Often, babies will at first use an object as a tool in an incorrect way. This is due to a combination of having realised the object (a key, for instance) has a function, but making erroneous assumptions about the nature of that function. So he may correctly understand that the key is necessary for opening the cupboard door, but may not know how or why. He may spend a long time pulling the key in and out of the lock as if that action will somehow magically cause the door to open. Finally, perhaps simply by accident, he will turn the key to discover the door open at last, and next time he will remember the successful, key-turning solution. Imitation also plays an important role in tool use, as it is often by watching the actions of others that infants are first alerted to an object's potential role. Research has been able to demonstrate that even before their first birthdays, babies begin to understand that acting on one object can affect another. In a series of experiments, ten- to twelve-month-olds were presented with a toy placed on a cloth in the centre of a table. While the toy itself was out of the baby's reach, the corner of the cloth was easily within grasp. Even at ten months, the infants were able to work out that by pulling on the cloth, the toy would be brought within their reach.

LOOKING AHEAD **During the second year of life, toddlers begin to use their hands not only to explore the world and for play, but also to take control of their daily lives. They start trying to feed and dress themselves, for example, well before they have developed sufficient manual dexterity to do so properly. These skills have their origins in early infancy when babies attempt to hold their own bottles, but by toddlerhood they will try to hold a spoon and even endeavour to feed others. The toddler will also be seen endlessly striving to fasten buttons or put on socks. He is entering a new phase of development.**

SELF-FEEDING AND DRESSING As soon as your baby is on solid foods, you can encourage him to feed himself. At first he may show no interest in holding his own bottle, and may even make a point of occupying his hands elsewhere by playing with a toy, holding both hands together, or even putting his arms down by his sides. There is no doubt that even though the drive for independence exists from a very young age, at around four months the baby still very much enjoys being cared for, indeed totally pampered, by his parents! However, as he gets older and increasingly in control of his movements, the infant will start to show a strong desire to take over holding the bottle if you have already placed it into his mouth. When hand-to-mouth coordination starts to become perfected, your baby may frequently wish to be in control of events in his daily life.

Babies can be encouraged to partake in feeding themselves by being offered finger-sized pieces of solid foods, such as segments of fruit, pieces of broken-up cookies or little strips of toast made to look like lines of soldiers.

I'm getting better and better at doing things for myself. I'm learning how to use a spoon, and I keep trying to put my socks on by myself and button my cardigan. But why does it take me so much longer than mum, and why do I get things so wrong?

As you become more and more agile with your hands and feet, you can start doing a lot more for yourself. But simple things can take you twice or three times as long as they take mum or dad because not only do you have to work out careful plans of action, but coordinating several movements doesn't yet come automatically to you. Be patient, though. With lots of practice, you too will be able to do everyday things without even thinking about them.

Initially, he may simply play with the food, suck it, squash it and make a general mess without swallowing anything at all. But all this is good not only for giving him the opportunity to find out about feeding himself, but also to make mealtimes fun and promote a relaxed attitude towards eating. Getting angry at baby if he messes around when you are trying to feed him might lead him to develop negative associations between food and being scolded. With the increasing social pressures on ever younger children to watch what they eat and not be fat, parents should always endeavour to instigate a very healthy and comfortable attitude towards food from as young an age as possible.

Around eleven to fourteen months, infants start their attempts at self-feeding using a spoon or a baby fork. These first clumsy efforts can be quite entertaining for everyone involved – although parents should arm themselves with a well-stocked pile of bibs and paper towels! – and are often the first obvious signs to the parents that their baby is becoming a tool-user. Initially, the baby will grasp the spoon very awkwardly and may find it impossible to keep it horizontal. This is because the type of vice-like grip young infants use has been practised on toys such as rattles, hairbrushes or sticks – which need not be held at any particular angle. Because of the difficulties of manipulating a spoon correctly, the spoon may first be used more as a noise-making tool than a feeding implement, as it is repeatedly banged on to the tray, or into the middle of the food plate, sending pieces of food flying everywhere but into the spoon! With some patience and practice, however, the infant does learn to tilt and control the spoon better by using his wrist and adjusting his grip.

Yet the feeding puzzle is still far from being solved. The infant must now work out how carefully to aim the spoon into the dish so as to fill it with food. This is no easy task. Misfiring with the aim may tip the dish over completely. And even more infuriatingly, it doesn't matter how accurately baby manages to bring the spoon splashing down into the middle of the plate, it still doesn't result in actually getting any food on to the spoon. In order to manage all this simultaneously, the infant has to work out a careful plan of action that involves combining many of the things he has been learning separately about reaching, grasping and scooping. Furthermore, all the different actions must then be carried out in the right sequence, which includes opening the mouth and swallowing at the end of the whole process. Imagine the complex messages being sent from the brain to the arms, hands and mouth. It is very easy to get things a little wrong, which is why

The roles are reversed: this little fellow is not only learning about feeding, but also imitating the social role he sees his mum playing.

'Which hole is my arm meant to go through?' Although babies get knotted up when trying to dress themselves, they persist relentlessly to work out the complex sequence of actions involved.

babies seem to find self-feeding quite a struggle – and may end up with half their face, ears and hair covered in spinach or egg! After several attempts, you might find your little one resorting to using the spoon as a musical instrument while he uses his other hand to stuff food surreptitiously into his mouth.

Interestingly, one of the first indications of whether a baby is right- or left-handed is to see with which hand he tries to use a spoon. Research has shown that as early as eleven months, the baby will demonstrate a clear preference for feeding himself with one particular hand. Other than this, it isn't until about three years of age that clear-cut handedness can be detected.

Dressing is another skill that demonstrates the baby's new sophisticated level of movement and object control. With the emergence of the pincer grasp, the infant can make increasingly precise movements, but it isn't until he has understood something about using objects to accomplish a task that he is ready to apply his manual skills properly to doing this for himself. Unzipping, buttoning and even pulling socks on all require careful selection of the right manual movement which must then be applied with considerable accuracy. But more than that, for each of these tasks the child must coordinate different actions by each hand. So, to unzip he must hold and pull down with one hand, while pinching and pulling up with the other. To button a jacket he must use his pincer grasp with each hand to hold on to two separate and very different things (the button hole in one hand while threading or unthreading the button with the other). And while managing all this, the toddler must also look down at a rather awkward angle to his own chest to make sure he is guiding the button into the hole. We do this without thinking, but just stop and watch yourself next time you button a shirt or pull on a sock and you will be amazed to realise just how complex a task it must be for the little learner.

Self-dressing rarely emerges until the latter half of the second year or even later, and may at first take the form of a game whereby baby spends hours zipping and unzipping, buttoning and unbuttoning. He may even invite you into turn-taking in these captivating games. Such efforts should always be praised, even if they are totally unsuccessful, as they will spur your child on to perfect his skills. Parents can further encourage the increasingly independent behaviour by letting the toddler choose his own clothes before trying to put them on. It will give him a real sense of self-confidence and achievement.

Mum and dad keep putting my pictures up on the wall all over the house, and showing them off to their friends. I didn't think they were that good! Am I the next Picasso?

Your early scribbles are as precious to your parents as paintings in museums. They may not yet be very artistic, but for your mum and dad they are the first things you have created all by yourself, using your own initiative and imagination. It will take you a couple more years before you are actually able to represent something real in your drawings, but they don't care about that. To them, even the most abstract of squiggles is a pure masterpiece.

EARLY DRAWING AND WRITING As soon as parents notice their child's willingness to use tools, they naturally start offering them the means to draw. Crayon and paper actually have little meaning to a one-year-old, and he may show more interest in poking the crayon into small gaps, using it as a stick and scrunching up the paper than in bringing the two together to produce a drawing. At this age he doesn't easily perceive that his hand movement has created an interesting trace on the paper. But a little coaching from mum or dad can soon change this. Within a few weeks, he may become increasingly engrossed in the unique scribbles he can produce with each individual hand movement. He will also of course notice the excitement with which his efforts are received, and this will spur him on to draw with even more enthusiasm. One can almost trace the changing level of excitement in the infant's drawing. It may begin quietly with a smooth straightish line, then get more and more zig-zaggy before reaching a swirly crescendo of squiggles which end with the crayon being banged down on to the paper several times, flattening the tip irretrievably. Watching a little child draw can be very funny. They often get so engrossed that they become oblivious to their surroundings and may even vocalise happily with each hand movement.

While early drawings are generally interpreted as complex and imaginative representations of the world by admiring parents, it isn't until the age of about two and a half that children really begin to attribute meaning to their scribbles. This is often done post factum and it is hard to know if the infant really intended to draw a 'dog' or whether he decided it was a dog after the event. But once the drawing is given a meaning – however little it may actually resemble the attributed label – the child will stand by that meaning even as long as a week later. At first, these representational drawings are quite symbolic in nature, using very fixed stereotyped images for things or people. Thus, as we saw in an earlier chapter, a person will be drawn as a head and two legs (*page 49*); a house may be a pentagon; and a flower, one large circle surrounded by smaller ovals.

Surprisingly, early stereotypes such as these are shared by most children throughout the world. They may be a reflection of underlying developmental milestones at this age in both representational and manual ability. Early pictures are also almost exclusively two-dimensional, with little attempt to represent depth and distance, although dimension relationships are apparent quite early on. Daddy is drawn very much larger than baby, even if neither actually resemble a father and a baby! Furthermore, when he draws a picture, the three-year-old rarely has a fixed, clear drawing in mind. Rather, his final creation is often the outcome of reinterpretation somewhere along the way. So, for instance, what may start as a person may end up as the sun. This is a time when he will be especially sensitive to the feedback he is receiving as he draws, and you may find that an innocent encouraging comment from you such as: 'Oh, what a pretty flower!' may transform the direction of his drawing completely.

This toddler isn't yet a Michelangelo, but early attempts at drawing (scribbling!) are vital to later development.

At around the time that young children begin to create mean-ingful pictures rather than mere squiggles, they start to discrim-inate between writing and drawing. This is not to say that the two-and-a-half-year-old is ready to learn to write the alpha-bet. But he has been watching your hand actions when you write, and comparing them to his. He now begins to do pre-tend writing, and this is very different from drawing. Unlike drawing, which uses all sorts of different sweeping hand movements, pretend writing involves making a series of small marks, sometimes in a tentative line, lifting the pen off the paper at regular intervals.

So learning about the world of drawing goes well beyond simply improving the way the child holds a pencil. Rather, it is a rich area of development in which manual dexterity, planning, intentionality, pride and self-confi-dence play an important role.

My Developing Intelligence

Have you ever put a child-resistant lock on a cupboard door only to find that your eighteen-month-old is busy emptying its contents? Or watched an eight-month-old holding a toy in each hand and trying to pick up a third? Learning how to overcome such obstacles; remembering where things are or what happened yesterday; forming categories of objects by exploring their different properties; learning to count; making plans and solving problems — these are all ways in which infants and toddlers display their growing intelligence, and all involve coordinating many different parts of the brain.

Scientists have shown that infant brains are busier than adult brains! In infancy the brain develops more synaptic connections than later in life. Every time your infant sees a new object or hears a new sound, her brain will form new connections. Between four and twelve months, for example, the visual cortex lays down 150 per cent more connections than that of an adult. Later, between the ages of two and four years, synaptic density falls to adult-like levels by a process of pruning. Redundant connections made in the first few months of life are cut back, while other more specialised pathways are strengthened. The auditory cortex, which processes all the different sounds in our world — language, music, cars passing by and so forth — follows a similar timetable to the visual cortex, initially overproducing connections during the first year and subsequently pruning them back.

By contrast, in one of the parts of the infant's brain responsible for intellectual development, the prefrontal cortex, the density of connections does not peak until after the infant's first birthday, and the drop to adult-like levels only takes place progressively between ten and twenty years of age. So intelligence continues to develop throughout the years of childhood and even into late adolescence. But the growth and pruning of connections is not the only changing activity that occurs in the brain as it develops. Neurotransmitters (the chemical processes that enhance and inhibit brain activity), as well as brain metabolism (the

process by which the brain fuels itself by consuming glucose) also alter significantly over the course of development. During the period of rapid growth and learning, the infant's brain is more active and consumes far more energy than it does in middle childhood and adulthood. In general, this progressive reduction of activity in brain chemistry and brain metabolism is a sign that the child's brain is forming increasingly specialised pathways, enabling her to move, speak and carry out intelligent acts rapidly and efficiently. Pruning the pathways to retain the most specialised ones frees up the brain to make new connections when the child is faced with novel situations.

The development of human intelligence — memory, exploration, planning and problem solving — is fundamental during the first few years of life and points to the crucial role that a stimulating environment can play. Talk to your baby directly as often as possible. Sing to her, read her books, direct her attention towards interesting events, objects and people. Do all these things from the start, even before she understands you. She will let you know if your stimulation is effective by responding positively (kicking her feet) or negatively (crying when over-stimulated).

While there are many ways in which parents can help this process along, it is important to remember that in order to explore the world confidently, the infant needs to feel emotionally secure. Quite a lot of research now exists showing that securely attached children are several IQ points higher than emotionally insecure children. So the more confident your child is, the more focused and inquisitive she will become, giving her brain the opportunity to strengthen the pathways that govern the development of intelligence.

Of course, these developments go on inside your baby's brain, so they are less visible than progress in, say, walking and talking. It is clearly very rewarding to you when your encouragements yield a new word or motor skill. But remember, all the stimulation you are providing continually develops the intellectual capacities of your baby's brain. So when, for example, you laugh at your baby's persistent attempts to sink a hollow plastic duck in the bath only to see it pop up again, think of her as a little scientist using her intelligence to explore the laws of physics!

How does my memory develop?

I seem to have a library inside my head where I store some of my experiences. How does it work and why is it so important to remember things?

Memory is crucial to your intelligence because it is a means of encoding, and later recalling, past experiences in order to build up your knowledge of the world. It works a little like a library with two separate sections storing short-term and long-term memories. Though you're not aware of it, some of your earliest memories were formed before you were born, although these will soon be updated to reflect all the exciting new experiences you're having in the outside world.

HOW MEMORY WORKS Memory is the ability to register, retain and retrieve information about past experiences. We continually resort to our memories in order to respond appropriately to what we are seeing, feeling, hearing, smelling and touching. Our memory store is constantly being updated to reflect the changing demands of our social and physical environments. Memories are thus vital in helping infants make sense of strange situations, solve new problems and interact with the people they meet. Although we are often oblivious to the central role memory plays in governing our behaviour, our memories act as pointers to guide us through life. The same is true for babies, although it takes a long time for the infant memory store to build up.

Human memory is a very complex system, but in order to appreciate how the baby remembers, it is worth looking at this system a little more closely. Although we often confuse recognising and recalling, they are actually quite different. Recognition occurs when you remember something as a result of experiencing or seeing that thing again. Recall, on the other hand, involves accessing from your mind a memory previously stored there. It can occur either as a result of a cue – an experience, a feeling, a smell or a sound which makes you remember something from your past – or spontaneously, simply remembering something out of the blue. There are two types of recall memory: autobiographical memory (what happened to you yesterday), and what is called 'semantic memory' which includes specific knowledge about the world (facts such as dogs are animals and tulips are flowers). There is also a third form of memory called 'procedural memory', which is built up as a result of acquiring skills.

All these different types of memories can be held simultaneously and accessed as a result of day-to-day experiences. So, for instance, when your baby crawls across the room, she makes use of her previous crawling experience in order to move her hands and legs efficiently (procedural memory); she recalls past events such as bumping into a wooden chair (autobiographical memory); and she remembers that wooden chairs are hard and sofas are soft (semantic memory). Accessing such memories influences her subsequent behaviour. These different types of memory skills are clearly very different and are in fact handled by different pathways in the brain, which take some time to develop and mature at different rates. Due to the immaturity of the young baby's brain pathways, up to two months of age infant memory is mainly based on recognition rather than recall. From then on, recall starts to develop and the baby is able to demonstrate a more sophisticated form of remembering.

Remembering is divided into two processes: one sends experiences to a short-term memory store where they are immediately processed, and the results of that processing are then sent to a long-term store where memories are created and retained for future use. The short-term memory capacity is very limited. That's why, if you're given a telephone number only once, you usually remember it just long enough to make the call or immediately write it down. In fact, short-term memories don't last longer than a second, which is why you usually have to rehearse the phone number even while you're picking up the receiver to start dialling. Information from the short-term memory which isn't left to decay is sent to the long-term memory for storage. So, writing the number down, visualising it and rehearsing it several times usually means you are able to recall it correctly at a later date. The long-term memory store is in principle unlimited and is essential for building up a working knowledge of the world. Furthermore, the memories stored therein can be retrieved over a lifetime as long as the right cues are used.

While this toddler's vocabulary is still limited, he can use actions to show his father that he remembers the picture on the wall that he saw yesterday.

Compared to adults, the amount of information infants can retain tends to be smaller and fades much faster; this is explored in detail in the next question. Nonetheless, although infants' capacity is limited, the different systems that govern infant memory are very similar to those of the adult. In other words, basically the same processes operate throughout life.

FORMING FIRST MEMORIES It is very hard for us to know just how much newborns and very young infants can remember. Scientists used to think that babies could not form proper memories until they developed language and the ability to categorise information in a coherent and communicable way. But a huge body of research has now shown that this is not the case, and that very early on infants not only exhibit the ability to remember objects, people and events, but also show evidence of remembering aspects of their life in the womb. As we saw in the

I'm only a few days old, but I can already remember certain things for very short periods of time. Will my memory span get longer as I grow bigger?

Although you pay close attention to everything in your surroundings, your memory is still fairly limited. However, it is quite impressive given how tiny you are and how few experiences you've actually had. Be patient, your memory capacity will grow very rapidly over the next few months.

chapter on language (*pages 76–107*), only hours after birth newborns already show a strong preference for both their mother's voice and their mother tongue, thanks to their experiences in utero. But as soon as they enter the world, babies begin to form new memories based on the multitude of experiences they have of sounds, sights, people, objects and events.

At first, each new memory a baby forms is very short-lived. In one experiment, for example, three-day-olds who heard a single new word repeated several times during the testing phase were able to recognise it only over a one-minute gap. Longer than that and the baby showed no signs of having heard the word before. At such a young age, the long-term memory stores are rather primitive, and new experiences can only be encoded at a very superficial and temporary level. With time, however, infants' memory skills improve and become more sophisticated. A whole series of interesting experiments have demonstrated the remarkable abilities of two-month-old infants to remember their experiences for up to two weeks. During the tests, each baby was placed in a cot with an interesting mobile hanging just above her. One of her legs was joined to the mobile with a long piece of ribbon, so that when she kicked, her movements caused the mobile to move also. After two weeks, the infant was tested again. Amazingly, if she was placed in the same cot, with the same mobile overhead, but without having her leg tied to it, she would kick vigorously in order to make the mobile move like the last time. She showed surprise when the mobile didn't move, indicating that she remembered the outcome of her actions two weeks previously. She also seemed taken aback if the designs on the mobile or the cot bedding were different. A group of similar-aged infants who had not taken part in the original experiment showed no kicking or surprise, indicating that the behaviour of the experimental group was really due to memory of the earlier event.

Memory for past experiences is initially very context bound. The experiments above indicated that at eight weeks infants needed to have their memory jogged by relevant cues (such as seeing the experimental cot again twenty-four hours before the second set of trials) in order to respond to the mobile after a gap of several days. They also remembered certain shapes on the mobile, like crosses, longer than they remembered L- or T-shapes, presumably

This young baby has little control over voluntary movement, but he shows his memory for the shapes on the mobile by vigorously kicking his legs.

Enhancing your baby's memory

There are many memory games you can play with your infant. Introduce your six-month-old to a new object and show her an unusual action with it. For instance, hold a small plastic cup in your hand and put it on your head several times. Then help her do the same, if necessary guiding her hand and the cup towards her head. Then put the cup away for a couple of days. When you next hand her the cup, see if she puts it on her head, which would indicate that she has recorded the event in her memory. (You can't use a drinking action because this is what she would normally do with a cup.)

Other favourite memory games that develop curiosity and intelligence involve hiding objects. Place a few coloured plastic cups upside down and hide a small object under one of them. Encour-age your six- to eight-month-old to lift the cups until she finds the object. Hide it again under a different cup. Make the game fun by asking, with lots of motherese intonation: 'Now, where's the little rabbit?' or 'Now where's the car?' This will stimulate her memory not only for location but also for object words. Once your child is crawling, put away her favourite toy in a particular box for a couple of weeks while she is looking. Then suddenly store the toy in a different box, again while she watches. Next, distract her with another activity for as long as you can, before asking her to find the toy again. See if she goes to the original box or whether she remembers the new storage place. Varying the ways in which you play with your baby will help you recognise the steps in her developing intelligence, so invent your own memory games. It will be fun for both of you.

because two intersecting lines are more salient than lines simply meeting. Memory for past events improves rapidly with age. By three months, babies are able to form far more coherent, detailed and long-lasting memories, which they can now retain for as long as eight days without the need to be reminded first. In fact, three-month-olds form memories for objects quickly and accurately. If they are presented with a series of colourful shapes on a screen, each appearing at a specific location in a set sequence, within minutes they are able to anticipate where the next object will appear, indicating that they have formed a memory of the spatial layout of the display.

Memory improves if we experience things through more than one of our senses. This is especially true for babies. So, an infant is far more likely to remember a toy if she has been able to touch as well as merely to see it, because she can form a memory that includes details about the toy's shape and the way it feels instead of just its colour and outline (*see also pages 169–71*). Even though memories seem to fade and disappear, infants actually store a memory of all experiences. The problem lies in how to retrieve them voluntarily in adulthood because they are bound to specific elements of that experience, such as a sound or smell that we may not experience again.

Memory for actions also develops dramatically as the infant is increasingly able to take an active role in events (rather than simply watching them). From ten months onwards, infants show a clear ability to remember complicated sequences of actions one week after having participated in them. For example, if a baby learns how to make a rattling toy by placing a coin into a box, closing it, and then shaking the box, she will repeat this sequence several days later when presented with a box and a coin, without needing to be shown the sequence again. By contrast, babies who simply watched an experimenter make the rattle did not remember the sequence as accurately. Thirteen-month-olds can correctly recall sequences involving up to four separate actions such as sitting a teddy bear in a chair, feeding the teddy, putting it to bed and covering the teddy bear with a blanket. A week after learning the sequence, they can reproduce it in the correct order, even if some of the props are changed, such as swapping the teddy bear for a Big Bird toy. So, not only have they formed detailed memories of the original event, but they are also able to organise these memories into logical but flexible sequences, making it possible for them intelligently to replace objects and actions as the need arises. This is of course why memory is so important to infants' developing intelligence.

Mum took me to the doctor yesterday and as soon as we went through the door I started crying and wanted to leave. What was it that frightened me?

It was your memory at work. You remembered your last encounter with the doctor when he gave you some particularly painful injections. So your tears show that you remember him and that he's not your favourite person! But you also remember the nice things about people and your interactions with them.

REMEMBERING ENCOUNTERS WITH OTHERS

The development of a baby's memory for people is crucial if she is to develop an understanding of the social world. We have already seen how rapidly the newborn stores information about her mother's face, voice and smell. Well, from early on in her life, her memory also extends to other people and to her interactions with them.

How does the prelinguistic child manage to tell us that she remembers someone or something? At only eight weeks, if she meets a new person who greets her by sticking his tongue in and out instead of saying 'Hello', she will demonstrate that she remembers their encounter by poking her tongue out next time she meets him, as if she were saying in their special way, 'Hello again, I've met you before.' She does not use this form of greeting with other people. At the first encounter, she formed a memory of her new friend which included not only what he looked like but also the way he behaved. It was this stored memory that was accessed the next time she saw him. Imitation of a social event is one of the only ways a baby can convey her memories before she can speak. Take the following example from a ten-

month-old. On a visit to grandparents, the infant saw a moth flapping against the window and she pointed the scene out to her father. He responded by saying: 'Yes, that's a moth. It's trying to get in.' On the next visit, the baby crawled over to the window, sat down, turned to her father and alternated between pointing to the window and flapping her hands, imitating the movements of the moth. It was as if she were saying: 'Remember last time, when we watched that moth trying to get in?' Likewise, if dad always has cereal for breakfast and one day starts with toast, a toddler may pass him the cereal box indicating that she remembers his usual habit. All of these memories can be conveyed without language.

The development of your baby's memory is generally very rewarding to watch, especially when she first shows a clear recognition of grandparents after a few weeks' absence. But it can occasionally be quite a nuisance to parents in a hurry. By the time your child reaches toddlerhood, her memory is becoming increasingly precise and expanding at a considerable rate. So, if you read the same story to your toddler every night, there will come a time when you are not allowed to skip a paragraph, change a single word, swap the order of events or stop too soon because she will be carefully monitoring your every word against her precise memory of the story. Better to choose a completely new story if you're short of time!

'Hey, I know you. You're the lady who always tickles my tummy.' This baby's confident smile shows she remembers her mother's friend.

How do I explore my surroundings?

Hey, that's interesting. My teddy bear seems to get smaller when mum takes it out of my cot, but I somehow know it's not shrinking as it moves away. Are my eyes playing some sort of trick on me?

No, your brain knows something that your eyes don't tell you. The image of the bear on your retina changes size as it approaches or gets further and further away from you, but your brain tells you that it's the same bear throughout. You have what is called size and shape constancy. This helps you understand the world of objects.

Eyes and coloured spots are particularly captivating to this young explorer.

WHAT BABIES CAN SEE   The visual system develops very rapidly after birth. While experience is important for stimulating the sense of sight, the development of visual acuity – the ability to bring things into focus – depends mainly on maturation of the eye and the visual cortex (the area of the brain involved in processing information from the eye), and takes years to reach the adult level. If a baby is born one month prematurely, she will have four weeks' more experience of the visual world than a full-term newborn. Yet despite this extra experience, the premature baby's visual acuity is no better than that of the newborn, suggesting that maturation of the brain plays an important role.

A newborn's vision is very limited as far as distance is concerned. Eyesight is measured by determining the distance at which small letters can be read. Whereas perfect sight is called 20/20 vision, newborn vision is only 20/500, which means that the baby's focusing distance is only about 4 per cent that of adults. By six months, this has improved to 10 per cent (or 20/200), and by twelve months her vision, now 20/50, is approaching adult levels – but in fact it is not until four to five years of age that children's vision reaches the full adult level. Of course, visual acuity differs significantly from one individual to another, so some infants may later need spectacles.

We have seen in earlier chapters how all the cells in the brain are present at birth but that the network of connections between cells is mainly built up during postnatal development. This is why the newborn initially responds better to details in her visual environment that are processed by the firing of *single* cells. In the visual cortex, specific single cells detect edges, straight lines, contours, bars, angles and contrasts. So the newborn is attracted to patterns with high contrast (black and white), well-defined shapes, large patterns and sharp edges. Furthermore, below the age of three months, infants can't discriminate all colours – they prefer longwave colours (red and yellow) over shortwave colours (blue and green), and they always prefer colours over grey.

Stimulating your baby's sense of vision

Because of the way infant vision develops, your baby's attention will be captured by different objects as she grows. Initially, sharp black-and-white patterns will be more interesting than soft pastel colours, so make sure your baby has both to look at. You may be surprised to find that her attention is captivated more by a chess board lying on the coffee table than by the expensive green cuddly toy you just gave her! At three months, babies also attend to differences between sharp and gradual changes in luminance, which help them gain information about the form of objects and where they are in space – so if your house has a dimmer switch, you can attract baby's attention by changing the lighting of a room. Don't forget, too, that early on some colours, like yellow, are easier to see than others, such as blue. Baby will also be particularly stimulated by moving objects, so rather than merely showing her a toy, bring it to life by jiggling it across her visual field and pretending it is speaking to your baby in response to her movements.

Prior to the onset of binocular vision (being able to integrate two-dimensional information from the two eyes), infants under three months use what is called 'motion parallax' in order to gain extra cues for distance and depth. This is because moving the head slightly produces apparent movement in the baby's whole visual field, causing objects nearby to appear to move more than those further away. You can enhance your baby's visual development by putting two fairly large objects on a table, one within her reach and the other several inches further behind. Place your baby on your lap facing the two objects and watch whether she moves her head slightly from side to side while looking at them. If she does, she is using motion parallax to ascertain which of the two objects is reachable. If she doesn't make these movements spontaneously, move her head very slightly from side to side yourself. If she makes the correct distance judgement, she will try to touch the nearer object and successful contact may encourage her to use motion parallax again.

Newborns pay particular attention to moving objects, especially things that move in their peripheral vision. Thus, if they are watching something in the centre of their visual field and they see something move in the corner of their eye, they turn towards the moving object. However, their ability to track moving objects across the visual field is still very slow and jerky. By six to eight weeks, this ability has developed considerably: the baby anticipates the motion of the object by achieving smoother and more continuous head and eye movements in order to keep the object in view. Anticipation is a crucial aspect of the development of intelligence and problem solving because it enables the infant to plan her action in advance of executing it.

When newborns scan a stationary object, at first they concentrate on one part of the contour. For instance, if they are shown a square, they may fixate on just one corner of it and would therefore have difficulty differentiating a square from a triangle (whereas they would have no problem seeing the difference between a square and a circle). By six to eight weeks they can scan the whole of the contour but begin to pay more attention to internal details. After three months, infants' visual scanning becomes more integrated, taking account of both the contour and the internal details, which enables them to build more complete representations of visual stimuli.

But vision entails far more than merely bringing objects into focus and building a representation of what they look like. Firstly, it involves 'size and shape constancy'. This means that although things look bigger when they are closer, you know that they haven't changed size. Likewise, as a CD case is rotated, its shape seems to change from a square to a long thin rectangle and then back to a square as the rotation is completed. But again you know that the object's shape has actually remained constant throughout. The visual system processes size and shape constancy accurately from birth. So when you bring a toy from the end of the cot to your baby's nose, the optical image of the toy on the infant's retina gets bigger and bigger, but research has shown that she knows that the toy did not grow in size nor change shape as it moved towards her.

Once an infant can turn each page to reveal the interesting pictures, baby books provide stimulation to the developing visual system, even at this very young age.

Although an understanding of size and shape constancy is present at birth, knowledge of depth and distance is not. This develops as a result of experience and changes in the structure of the eye. The main clue available to the eye for judging depth is stereopsis – the process of integrating into a single image what each eye sees. Our visual system does this automatically, but to experience this clever faculty, take a look at the picture on this page, close one eye and note what you see. Then open it and close the other eye, and note the difference between the two visual experiences. With both eyes open, the two separate images merge into a single one: because each eye is seeing the picture from a slightly different angle, the visual system calculates the distance from the eyes to the picture. But babies under ten weeks do not have stereopsis. It is almost as if they have tunnel vision in each eye – somewhat like double vision – so the information provided to the brain by the left eye is not integrated with that provided by the right eye. Thus if a young infant were to close one eye and look at this page, then repeat this with the other eye, with both eyes open she would still see these as separate images rather than a merger of the two. Stereopsis is important for three-dimensional vision. But this doesn't mean that young infants see only two-dimensionally, because prior to stereopsis they may get some 3-D cues from shading, texture and from moving their heads to change their visual angle on an object. However, once infants achieve stereoptic vision, their view of the world changes radically. They can locate the position, size and shape of objects more precisely. This is when we start to witness the coordination of reaching and seeing, so important to their developing intelligence.

USING THE EARS From the sixth month in utero, pathways in the auditory cortex in the brain are already forming and by birth the infant's hearing has many of the complexities of an adult's. Newborns respond to a wide range of sound frequencies (pitch) and intensities (loudness), but this improves even more after the first few days in the outside world, once the fluid has dissipated from the ear canals.

Sounds of every kind fill the baby's environment – voices, rattles, telephones, music, cars, the turning of pages, running water, the unzipping of clothes – and we use sound stimulation to attract her attention and develop her intelligence. Experiments have shown that newborns discriminate more accurately between certain sounds, for example white noise and pure tones. White noise is like the sound you hear when the television channel is not tuned, for instance, and all the sound frequencies are equally intensive; pure tones are simple auditory structures such as each single note produced by a flute. Although newborns find these sounds easiest to process, they actually show a strong preference for the sound of human voices, which are much more complex (being made up of multiple frequencies and intensities) but more rewarding. Another complex sound particularly attractive to the newborn is music. Although infants like all forms of music, recent studies have shown that newborns prefer music accompanied by singing voices. Furthermore, fretful babies always prefer sound stimulation – lullabies, reassuring words, the beating of a metronome – to silence.

In the past, hearing problems often went unnoticed until the age of about three. Nowadays, researchers and doctors use various measures to determine whether a baby is responding to sound: increases in the heartbeat and kicking,

I can't see things in the dark. So why do I turn my head towards the door before mum opens it?

It's because you can hear mum's footsteps approaching and you can tell where the sound is coming from. So you look towards the direction of the sound in the hope that mum will appear out of the dark and take you into her arms. Your little ears are already very sensitive and the noises that fill your world are helping you make sense of your surroundings.

The world of sound is fascinating. This toddler is discovering how music and voices can come out of an inanimate box.

eye blinking, the startle reflex, changes in the sucking rate, head turning and changes in electrical activity in the brain. This is important because early intervention can have dramatic effects on improving an infant's sensitivity to language and other auditory input before more serious problems set in. The newborn's reaction to sound is much slower than that of an older child or adult. It can take up to six or eight seconds for an infant to show overt responses to a noise, although the brain begins to process the sound much sooner. But by the middle of the first year the baby takes only about two or three seconds to show a response. It will be another year before the infant's capacities almost reach those of an adult, although myelination (*page 31*) of the auditory pathways actually continues well into the fourth year of life.

Infants use sound to locate objects they cannot see. The question is whether the newborn who reacts to a noise is simply turning towards sound as a reflex, or actually turning to find the object from which the sound emanated? Researchers continue to disagree on this point because the latter involves higher-level cognitive processes whereby the infant would have to understand that sounds come from things, rather than simply being disembodied. Interestingly, between two and three months there is a tendency for babies to become less responsive to sound stimulation – this is the time when voluntary reactions are taking over from more reflex-like ones. By three to four months, however, it is clear that infants expect objects to make noises and they become increasingly precise at locating sounds. They look more intently at the correct location of the sounding object rather than in the general vicinity of the object, and they begin to reach for it more accurately.

There are many similarities between the development of the hearing and visual senses. For example, like the data about depth provided by each eye (stereopsis, *see page 164*), clues from each ear supply vital information as well. Each ear hears a sound at a slightly different intensity, which gives the brain information about the direction and distance from which the sound emanates. The ability to integrate these two sources of auditory information develops during infancy, and by about sixteen to eighteen months a baby's skill at discriminating tiny shifts in sound is like that of an adult. So if you squeak a toy in a darkened room just in front of your baby's cot and then squeak it again a mere 20 degrees to the left, you will see her head move a tiny bit in that direction to locate the sound. Also, infants can discriminate between receding and approaching sounds (as they can visually) and by six months they know that the objects making the sounds are the same, despite changes in intensity. So the understanding of sound contributes to the child's understanding of the multiple properties that objects can have.

This four-month-old turns his head and uses sound correctly to locate the rattle his mother is shaking.

MOUTHING   As we saw in the first chapter, hand–mouth interaction begins in utero, allowing the foetus to experience tactile stimulation by sucking her thumb. At birth, mouthing is merely the combination of the Babinsky, rooting and sucking reflexes (*see pages 38–43*). The hand-to-mouth reflex involves the mouth opening in anticipation of the approaching hand. Mouthing is also very feeding-related initially. Research has shown that the presence of a sweet taste in the mouth, such as milk, is accompanied by an increase in the frequency with which babies bring their hands up to their mouths. However, mouthing soon progresses beyond anything to do with taste and feeding and becomes the infant's prime means of exploring objects at a time when the hands are still clumsy. Indeed, there are more nerve-endings in the mouth than in the

I know this toy car isn't part of my dinner, but it feels cold, smooth, curved and hard on my tongue. Why do I have this urge to put things into my mouth?

Your drive to 'mouth' objects is currently your best means of exploring objects and finding out about their texture, size, shape and temperature. Although it may seem rather primitive, it is actually an important milestone in the development of your intelligence.

fingertips during early infancy. The neural pathways relating to the tongue, lips and mouth are the first to develop in the cerebral cortex and these are therefore the most sensitive areas for examining objects.

Mouthing increases rapidly over the first six months of life and decreases as fine manual control improves. Even prior to the emergence of voluntary reaching, the infant will orally explore an object placed in her hand rather than first looking at or manipulating it. Through trial and error, the baby soon learns that some objects are more suitable for mouthing than others. For instance, furry, stringy items like teddy bears or human hair are easy to bury fingers into but not pleasant to fill the mouth with. Heavy or large objects either weigh too much or are too big to bring up to the mouth (although one solution is to bring the mouth to the object, so you will find your baby mouthing the side of the cot or the edge of a chair). But the prime candidates for mouthing are light, plastic or squishy objects. Interestingly, although more or less anything will be mouthed, research has shown that infants tend to mouth silent objects, such as the edge of a plastic plate, more than audible objects like rattles, which are better waved. This is because they are beginning to categorise objects and have realised that certain actions will lead to the discovery of different kinds of information, which creates new links in their brains.

At this stage of development, the lips and tongue offer so sensitive a means of exploration that it can provide your baby with a very accurate internal image of the object being mouthed – even if she hasn't actually seen the object. In one study, two-month-old babies were given either a dummy with a knobbly teat to suck, or one with a smooth teat. The babies did not see the dummies before they were put into their mouths, so the only information they could gain about the dummies was from mouthing. While they were sucking, they were shown two pictures simultaneously: one of the knobbly dummy, the other of the smooth one. Remarkably, the babies preferred to look at the picture that corresponded to the actual dummy they were sucking, showing that even mouthing can be an extremely rich source of information.

Just about anything can be mouthed! A small rattle, a book – and even a door frame. The mouth can reveal lots of important information about the features of objects.

I like playing guessing games in the dark with my toys before I drop off to sleep. I squeeze them and try to work out which toy I'm touching just by the sound it makes or how it feels in my hand. How come I so often prove to be right when I check things out in the light of day?

You have become very good at matching and integrating the different information that your hands, eyes and ears give you. This marks an important step forwards in the way your senses interact with one another to provide you with a far richer representation of objects in the world.

Now that the various senses are coordinated, the baby on the left can form a good representation of what this textured ball feels like, even though he's only been looking at it.

COORDINATING THE DIFFERENT SENSES So far we've looked at how each of a baby's senses – seeing, hearing, touch – develops separately, but in fact we rarely use a single sense when we encounter something new. We combine information from our eyes, ears, fingers and often our noses and mouths to build a complex, multi-dimensional representation of an object. This ability to coordinate information from two or more sources is known as 'cross-modal matching', and allows you, for instance, to identify an item visually that you had previously been able to touch but not see. Are babies born with this ability, or is it something that takes time to develop?

Although the visual, auditory and tactile senses certainly become increasingly coordinated with age, early signs of cross-modal matching, such as matching two dots on a computer screen to two drum beats, are difficult to interpret. Some researchers believe they involve true matching from the visual to auditory modalities or vice versa. Others argue that the newborn may represent the information she obtains from her different senses into a single, identical, abstract mental image which would not require cross-modal matching. However, once the infant is beyond two to three months and carrying out voluntary exploration, most researchers agree that this does involve the integration of different senses.

Although visuo-tactile coordination is involved in mouthing between two and three months, it is not until between four and eight months that the baby's fingertips are sensitive enough for her to be able to equate what she feels in her hands with what she sees. Such matching enables her to develop richer representations of objects. In one study, four-month-old infants were presented with an object that they could not see but that they could explore with their

After a few weeks' crawling experience, this nine-month-old has become aware of depth, and approaches the edge of the bed with caution.

hands under a blanket. One group of infants was given a pair of rings joined by a flexible string, while the other group was given rings joined by a rigid rod. The difference between the two stimuli was that the first seemed to be two objects that could move independently of one another in each hand, whereas the other formed a rigid, single object. After exploring the objects under the blanket, the infants were shown two visual displays, one picturing two rings separated in space and the other picturing two rings joined by a straight bar. Once again, infants displayed amazing intellectual capacities by looking longer at the display that corresponded to what they had felt with their hands, correctly matching vision and touch.

The growing use of the hands in the second half of the first year as a means of exploration and control over the environment, together with improvements in locomotion through crawling, lead to further discoveries in the infant's development. For example, researchers have for a long time examined the infant's reaction to changes in depth by using what is called the 'visual cliff'. A transparent surface covers an area of checked pattern, which is made to look as if it has a shallow end and a deep end. The baby's reactions to being above the shallow and the deep ends are compared. Before the onset of crawling, the baby shows no fear of being above the deep end. But once she is moving by herself, she displays reluctance to cross over the visual cliff and crawl above the deep end, despite her mother's encouraging calls and the fact that she is crawling on a solid surface throughout. In other words, once she has developed a sophisticated understanding of depth and uses this to guide her locomotion, she is able to override simple tactile information (the fact that her hands tell her brain that the surface remains constant) in favour of the more important cues derived from what her eyes tell her brain (that a danger may be present). Not only are her senses now beginning to really work together, but she is able to order them hierarchically as the situation demands.

How do I make sense of the world?

UNDERSTANDING OBJECT PERMANENCE

When a seven-month-old infant tries to reach for an attractive toy which is then covered with a cloth, she will retract her arm and stop trying to get the toy. This observation led psychologists to presume that until the end of the first year infants have no concept of 'object permanence': that an object continues to exist even when it has disappeared from sight. In the past decade, however, a series of ingenious experiments has seriously challenged this assumption, since it has now been shown that under some circumstances even three- to four-month-olds understand something about the continued existence of hidden objects. It appears that the early experiments were too dependent on reaching abilities – which, as we saw in the previous chapter, take time to develop – instead of tapping into the baby's capacity to make inferences about object permanence. So the new research focuses on the 'looking behaviour' (*see page 16*) of babies as young as three to four months, rather than waiting until they can display reaching behaviour.

In order to test early sensitivity to object permanence, four-month-olds were shown a locomotive moving along a track, which then disappeared behind a screen and reemerged on the other side. After seeing this event

Mum takes my teddy bear out of my cot when I go to sleep at night. I used to get a little scared that he'd gone for good, but now I seem to know he hasn't disappeared forever. How come I understand that things I can't see still exist?

You're learning something fundamental about the world: that things persist in time and space even when they are out of view. Just as you don't disappear when mum turns her back to you to get a nappy, so objects and people that go out of sight continue to exist. Of course, there are some things that do disappear forever – like a burst soap bubble – but through experience you'll learn which things are permanent and which are not.

This seven-month-old is engrossed in playing with his rattle. But once it is covered with a towel, he immediately loses interest, believing his out-of-sight toy has disappeared.

several times, the screen was removed and, while the baby was watching, a large wooden cube was either placed across the newly exposed part of the track, blocking the train's future passage, or next to the track leaving the passage free. The screen was now replaced, hiding that part of the track. The train was then made to start its journey again, and in both cases it completed its journey. Babies who had watched the cube being placed across the track showed surprise at the train's successful passage, suggesting that they had expected the hidden cube to remain an obstacle to the train. Even though they could no longer see the cube once the screen was in place, they nonetheless maintained a representation of the cube and its position and predicted its effect on the train's trajectory. So out of sight is not out of mind, even at this very early age.

The ability to trace objects in space and time, despite their momentary disappearance, is a crucial property of understanding the way the physical and social worlds behave. Imagine if each time an infant's mother left the room, she thought her mum had disappeared into thin air! The fact that the baby can represent her mother, and hold on to that representation when she is not present, is fundamental in building up stable ideas about her environment. Such representations may initially be quite crude, but they are the basis of her subsequent intellectual development.

With time, infants' representations become more elaborate such that they can encode quite complex features of events. By seven months, babies analyse objects along many dimensions. They notice size, texture, shape and colour, and predict the behaviour of objects according to specific features. This is important for object permanence. The baby now not only represents an object as there or not there, but also infers how it will behave out of sight – that is, she will assume its properties will persist under all circumstances. So infants expect a hard, wooden cube to remain solid and unsquashable, even when hidden by a screen, and will show surprise if the screen seems to flatten the cube. By contrast, they won't show surprise if it is a sponge that gets flattened by the screen. Object permanence also allows them to maintain representations about size and shape so as to compare objects out of sight. So if a marble rolls across the floor and out of view, the infant will expect it to come out again from under the sofa. But she will anticipate a rubber ball to behave differently. Holding information about size and compressibility in mind, she is able to judge which of the two objects will get stuck under the sofa. These examples may seem trivial to adults, but they illustrate the intellectual advances made during the second half of the first year.

By around nine months, it becomes easier for parents to notice their baby's increasingly sophisticated knowledge about object permanence because it can be illustrated by their reaching behaviour rather than solely their looking behaviour. At this age, the infant will lift a cloth to reveal a toy that has just been hidden there. However, once they have been successful in finding the toy in this particular location, they will keep looking in the same place even when the toy is visibly moved to a new hiding place – they cannot inhibit the earlier successful response they learned. Of course, if they then see it repeatedly hidden in the second place, they won't make this error. This well-known behaviour is called 'the A not B error' and has attracted a plethora of research activity. It is now known that memory plays a role in the infant's erroneous reaching. If the baby reaches for a toy immediately upon seeing it being moved, she is more likely to pick the correct hiding place than if she waits several seconds. As infants get older, they can tolerate longer time delays between hiding and reaching – another sign of their growing intelligence.

By their second year, infants are not only able to follow visible displacements, such as moving a big toy from one box to another, but they can also make inferences about *invisible* displacements. So if a toddler watches a hand go into a box where a tiny toy is hidden, and then the hand picks the toy up and moves it to another hiding place, then the infant will immediately look in the new location. She makes this inference even though she only saw the hand move and not the toy itself, because it was small enough to fit into the closed hand. This understanding of invisible displacement marks the culmination of 'object permanence' and new developments in problem solving.

You can't pull the wool over this baby's eyes. By nine months, his knowledge of object permanence allows him to work out that his toy is still there even when it has been hidden under a blanket.

That can't be right. The train dad bought me just moved on its own. Is it magic or did someone push it when I wasn't looking?

Your toy train has a wind-up key, which is why it seemed to move without needing a push. But you're right to be surprised. Objects don't usually self-propel. You're rapidly discovering that this is one of the key differences between the behaviour of objects and that of people or animals, which move on their own.

LEARNING ABOUT THE LAWS OF PHYSICS

Getting to know the principles of object behaviour is one of the vital steps in your infant's understanding of the physical laws that govern our world. One of these principles, for instance, stipulates that a solid object cannot pass through another solid object. Three-month-olds display their sensitivity to this fact by showing surprise if they see a scene on a video screen that depicts a ball magically passing through the surface of a table. From six months, babies understand something about gravity. So if a ball is thrown from a height and magically stops mid-air before reaching the floor, an infant's behaviour shows that her expectations have been violated. By seven months they can predict that gravity will have an effect on the speed of a toy car travelling up or down a hill. They expect the car to roll progressively faster as it comes down. All this knowledge is called upon by the infant whenever she encounters a new situation.

Another aspect of the infant's growing knowledge of the physical world involves the relationship between cause and effect. As adults we know that when we play pool, the impact of one ball (A) on another (B) will make ball B move. Imagine your surprise if ball B were propelled forwards before ball A hit it. Similarly, it would make no sense to you if, upon impact, ball B were to pause for a moment before moving. Infants as young as six months have the same expectations about the outcome of impact between two objects. They have understood something fundamental about the spatial and temporal constraints that dictate the cause-and-effect relations between objects.

Everyday activities such as taking a bath or sitting in a high chair provide the baby with plenty of opportunities to make interesting and fun discoveries about the laws of physics. For instance, she will discover that if she drops her hollow plastic duck into the bath it will float on the surface of the water and will not stay under water even if she pushes it down to the floor of the bath. A bar of soap, on the other hand, will behave very differently. Infants can spend hours

Does your baby understand cause and effect?

Although babies make inferences about object relations well before the onset of language, these are not obvious to parents and can be demonstrated only through scientific experiments. But once infants start to speak, they can actively display to others their growing awareness of the world of cause and effect. Parents can follow the development of their child's understanding by watching for changes in her use of language. Most children first produce words referring to objects and people: 'mum', 'bottle', 'ball' and 'dog'. These are just labels. In order to communicate something about their primitive knowledge of the behaviour of things, they need to use action words. So, when your child begins to use words such as 'gone' or 'bye-bye' (like the little girl waving goodbye in the photograph) you can take this as a sign that she is intentionally telling you about her understanding of object permanence. Similarly, words like 'broken' and 'cut' may be used to indicate changes in state, while words like 'falled' and 'over there' mark changes in location. Finally, some children use words like 'oh-no' to mark a thwarted problem-solving attempt and words like 'gottit' to mark success in, say, building a tall tower with several building blocks. At around two years of age, this explodes into a plethora of 'why?' questions, as we shall see on pages 188–9.

experimenting in this way. So when they persist in throwing everything over the side of the high chair or out of the cot, or when they bang their spoon on a glass or a bottle, they're not being naughty: they're merely fulfilling their roles as little physicists!

Through both observation and exploration, babies also discover the principle of balance. For example, seven-month-olds are capable of assessing whether one cube placed on top of another will balance or fall, based on how much of the top cube is touching the surface of the bottom one. Incredibly, babies can appreciate the relationship between an object's position and its centre of gravity. If, by trickery, one cube is made to balance on top of another with only a tiny part of their surfaces touching, a baby looking at it will show surprise, indicating that she expected the top cube to fall. But at this age infants can only assess the balance relationships of simple, symmetrical objects like building blocks: even nine-month-olds show no surprise if an asymmetrical object such as a spoon (which is heavier at one end than the other) doesn't fall off a supporting surface when it should do. It takes several more months before they realise that an object's centre of gravity does not always lie above the geometric centre of the length of the object. This understanding probably comes from their greater experience in handling and playing with different-shaped construction toys.

*I think I'm turning into a robot. I keep
trying to copy everything mum does. Don't
I have a mind of my own?*

*Imitating the behaviour of those around you is an
indication that your mind is becoming more and more
sophisticated. You are both communicating and
learning every time you mimic an action, facial
expression or vocalisation that your parent produces.
Far from being robotic, imitation shows that you can
understand and predict the behaviour of others and
have learned important things about the relationship
between yourself and other people.*

*'Your turn, my turn, your turn.'
It's not that easy to imitate, so
this baby's attempts to copy
mum's peek-a-boo ends in fits
of giggles.*

IMITATION   From an early age, babies begin to
mimic the behaviour of those around them. This not
only forms an important part of social interaction,
but also plays a vital role in learning and problem
solving, helping the infant acquire new knowledge
and skills. Imitation allows her to learn new behaviours that she has not produced spontaneously. For
instance, an infant may watch her father hammering
a picture hook into the wall and then start banging
her rattle on the wall herself, even though she does
not understand the function of the original act. Such
imitatory actions may lead to fortuitous discoveries
and enable the infant to associate the act and its outcome for use in new problem-solving strategies.

Imitation plays an important role as an index of
an infant's growing theory of mind and indicates new
understanding about the relationships between self
and others. By imitating her mother's peek-a-boo
game, the baby shows that she understands her
gestures, that she can duplicate her actions, and that
she can predict that her reciprocal behaviour will have
similar meaning to her mother. But this is only part of
the picture. The process also involves complex, cross-
modal coordination between the pathways in the
brain that govern action and those that govern
thought. In order successfully to imitate an action like
opening the mouth wide, the baby has to map the
movements she sees on her father's face on to an
action plan that helps generate her own motor output. Likewise, she has to learn how to relate the look
of her father's mouth shape to her own, which she can
feel but not see. She also has to gauge her father's intentions and mirror these.
Imitation thus involves the infant recognising that other people are like her
in both mind and body.

Due to the complex cognitive processes involved in imitating,
researchers disagree as to whether newborns and babies up to two months
are really able to mimic someone intentionally or whether they are simply
displaying reflex-like behaviour. Many scientists have argued that newborns
lack the higher cognitive capacities required to form mental representations
and imitate voluntarily. They believe early imitative behaviour is reflex-driven

and not fully intentional. Only moments after birth, the newborn may stick her tongue out or open her mouth wide if her parent does the same. She may even copy her parent's head movements from side to side. But these actions all form part of her normal behavioural repertoire and are also produced in response to a number of other kinds of stimulation. For instance, she may poke her tongue out when she sees a pen protruding in and out of a tube or move her head in response to the interesting visual changes that the pen's movement produces. Clearly, at this very early stage, she is not necessarily behaving in this way to communicate: 'Look! I can do what you can do.'

Nevertheless, parents are encouraged to try imitation games with their very young babies. Poking your tongue out, opening your mouth and eyes wide, moving your head from side to side, and opening and closing your fists while your baby watches intently all provide her with exciting stimulation and may elicit similar behaviour from her. Irrespective of whether these interactive exchanges involve true mimicking, they are reward-ing for both of you and help to generate new connections in your baby's brain.

The development of imitation progresses through a num-ber of stages. Between three and four months, when true imitation emerges, the infant tends mainly to copy those actions she produces naturally in her day-to-day life. The further a behaviour is removed from her daily repertoire, the harder it is to imitate. Take the example of tongue protrusion. This is imitated enthusiastically early on, probably because it forms part of the newborn's rooting and sucking reflexes. If you play a game of sticking your tongue out at your baby, she may spend five minutes copying you, during which she will become better and better at it. By four months, however, the baby is less interested in imitating this gesture because it is being replaced by more inten-tional behaviours such as trying to produce sounds. She will now be more easily enticed to imitate hand clapping or screwing up her nose, because she can do these voluntarily.

By eight months the infant begins to imitate unfamiliar actions. In fact, during the next six months, she will be more interested in copying new behav-iours than old ones, and will concentrate on those actions that are pertinent to the situation she finds herself in. So it may now be difficult to make your twelve-month-old infant clap her hands or wave her arms if she is busy arrang-ing her toys in a line. Much better to encourage her to imitate, for instance, touching each object in sequence as though she were starting to count.

Imitation is far from automatic. This baby's concentration is very apparent as he tries to reproduce his mum's clapping.

Between six and twelve months, imitation becomes not only more complex but also increasingly accurate, and the infant is able to reproduce a behaviour almost exactly as she sees it.

Somewhat older, the toddler will learn to stand on a little stool in the bathroom by watching mum demonstrate this, integrating the new behaviour into her problem-solving strategies. If, say, she covets a cookie on the table but mum is out of the room, she may turn a box upside down and stand on it to increase her height. Imitation also allows the child safely to explore issues involving social interaction through pretend play. The toddler may act out with toys a quarrel she has witnessed between her parents in an attempt to make sense of the experience. This too is problem solving. So imitation contributes not only to the discovery of problem-solving strategies, but also to the exploration of issues involving social interaction.

Delayed imitation occurs between fourteen and eighteen months. At this stage, toddlers are able to produce accurate copies of actions, such as witnessing mum brushing the dog's tail the previous day. There is no need now to practise the imitative act: it is precise on first attempt 24 hours or even several days later. This is an important development because it requires the ability to store the information internally, to access that mental representation at a later date, and then to translate the stored image of another's behaviour into an action. What seems simple to an adult turns out to require a whole range of complex and interrelated brain processes.

CREATING CATEGORIES It is very difficult to ascertain the precise age at which babies begin to sort the things in their world into different classes. Categorisation is an important and very useful skill. It allows the infant to accumulate and process information faster and more efficiently, especially when she is faced with new situations. By storing information categorically, she reduces the need to relearn things over and over again. Imagine how difficult life would be if, every time we saw a different car, we had to relearn that a car is a vehicle, has wheels, is made of metal and moves! It is by creating a category for 'car' that we can keep knowledge of this kind together and use it to analyse all the different large, moving objects we see in the street.

Hmm, I've noticed that birds and aeroplanes look quite similar when they fly. So how come I can tell which is which so easily?

You know that birds are 'animals' and that aeroplanes are 'vehicles', and that these are two very different types of thing. Your brain creates categories to file away the knowledge you acquire in a clever and efficient way. This allows you rapidly to integrate new information and not to muddle things that look alike visually but are very different conceptually.

From a very young age, a baby begins to analyse her environment along several dimensions. At first she will note whether an object is self-propelled or needs to be pushed in order to move, what type of movement it makes, and what colour, general shape or texture it is. These characteristics allow the baby to form a number of global categories such as animal, vehicle and furniture with which to classify the world of things. For the animal category, global features might include: is self-propelled, has a furry texture and a face. The furniture category might cover properties such as: doesn't move, is solid, can be sat or leaned on. It is easy to see how the infant's early categories may be somewhat inadequate. Before the end of the first year, for example, babies do not have separate categories for animals like dogs and rabbits. It is not that they cannot *visually* distinguish between a variety of animals, it is simply that they do not *conceptually* categorise them as different.

Global-level categories like animal, vehicle, and male or female are part of the infant's intellectual tools as early as seven months. Experiments have demonstrated that from this age onwards, infants classify series of pictures of objects or animals by using the principle that they are 'the same sort of thing'. They also successfully treat non-members of each category differently – that is, they look longer if a non-member follows a series of category members. As infants get older, their actions become clues to their categorisation behaviour. Ten- to twelve-month-olds given an array of small yellow plastic animals and vehicles to play with will examine sequentially all those that belong to the animal category before they start to explore those belonging to the vehicle category. If you hand a one-year-old a series of plastic animals, one after another until you reach a yellow plastic bird with outstretched wings, and next hand her a yellow plastic aeroplane, she will

Having formed a category for 'vehicles', the toddler will no longer bang a toy car on a surface but will select an appropriate action for that toy, like rolling.

suddenly spend more time playing with the aeroplane as if to indicate that you have changed categories. What is particularly interesting is that a small yellow plastic plane is visually very much like a small yellow plastic bird. But the infant is not fooled: she makes the bird hop along the floor and tweet, and may even feed it with pretend water, whereas she holds the aeroplane above her head to fly or makes it move along the table smoothly like a vehicle. She never pretends to feed the aeroplane or makes engine noises for the bird. Her distinctive behaviour with each toy indicates that she places the bird in the animal category and the plane in the vehicle category. So, from about twelve months onwards, categorisation is not based on visual attributes but on the meaning or function of an object. This enhances the infant's storage of knowledge.

During the second year, the infant begins to form more complex classifications. The very wide category of vehicle can now be subdivided into more precise categories such as car, cycle and lorry. Similarly, the animal category can be divided into dogs, cats, horses and so forth. Soon, even more refined categories are developed, such as alsatian versus poodle, or lorry versus bus. To reiterate an earlier point, the toddler has been able to see the difference between a lorry and a bus since early infancy; what has changed is that her behaviour is no longer governed by *perceptual* differences but by classifications based on *conceptual* differences. Finally, around 20–24 months, the onset of the vocabulary spurt provides the child with labels for her categories, so that she is now able to communicate to others how she is interpreting and categorising her world. From this point on, toddlers become avid little 'sorters', trying to fit each new encounter into a pre-existing category or creating new ones to catalogue their ever-expanding worlds.

One teddy bear, one doll, one rattle. Hey, that's the same number of things as one apple, one orange, one banana. I haven't had a single maths lesson, so how do I know this?

After only a few weeks of life in the outside world, you've already gained a certain amount of counting knowledge. Humans, like many other species, are born with a predisposition for quantifying, and you're just discovering the beginnings of this special ability. It will be invaluable to you throughout life, and even at this very primitive stage it's already helping you make sense of your environment.

LEARNING TO COUNT Numbers are the means by which the things in our lives can be quantified. They also help us to process, classify and categorise information that reaches our brains. As such, numerical knowledge is an essential part of daily life. And this is not only the case for human beings: many other species of animals and insects also possess a means of counting in order to keep track of numbers of predators, sources of food, members of a pack and so on. Although most of the time we are unaware of their vital role, numbers permeate everything in our lives. Without them, we would have no way of working out baby's age, measuring the right amount of ingredients for baby's next meal, nor calculating how many nappies are left before needing to do the next shop. And there would be no understanding of the monetary exchange required to purchase them. Without numerical knowledge, the world would be chaotic. This also obtains for the infant. From early on, quantification plays an important role in the way she processes her environment. Not surprisingly, therefore, signs of a rudimentary understanding of numbers can be seen in the behaviour of babies as young as three months of age.

As we have seen in previous chapters, the human infant is born with the predisposition to attend to complex visual and auditory stimulation. From the moment she is born, her attention is attracted to sights and sounds that contain many interesting contrasts and changes. Very quickly she learns to discriminate between displays with few details versus many. By three months, the infant is able to demonstrate that she has learned something important about the difference between one, two and three. She knows nothing about the words 'one', 'two' and 'three', or the symbols that represent these words (1, 2, 3), but she already understands that a group of three dolls contains the same number of items as a group of three teddy bears. She also discriminates between one object and a set of two or three objects. But at such a young age, she cannot tell the difference between a set of three items and sets of four, five, six or more. It seems that, until some time around the age of 24 months, the human infant's capacity to process numbers is restricted to amounts of three or below. Nonetheless, as early as five months, the baby's numerical knowledge has become sophisticated enough to allow her to make very rudimentary calculations such as 1+1=2, and 3−1=2. All this before she is able to say, let alone read or understand, the actual words 'one', 'two' or 'three'!

In order to discover something about the infant's secret knowledge of numbers, scientists have had to devise clever experiments using the sucking and looking-time techniques with which you are now familiar. By recording subtle changes in the baby's sucking rate or the amount of time she looks at one display over another, researchers have established new facts about three-month-old abilities. At this young age, the baby already forms strong expectations about what she is seeing or hearing, based on her numerical sensitivity. For instance, if she is shown a series of interesting displays on a computer screen, all containing three items (three flowers, then three cars, three balloons and so on), and very occasionally a set of two items (two flowers or two balloons) appears unexpectedly, she will suck harder on the dummy or look longer at the screen whenever the number in the display changes. The baby's behaviour tells us two things. By reacting in similar ways every time she sees a three-item display,

At ten months, this little girl cannot interpret the number symbols on these blocks. But she already knows that there are three blocks and that by picking one up, she leaves two behind.

THE BUDDING MATHEMATICIAN

An ingenious experiment has been devised to investigate very early mathematical abilities in the human infant. Placed in front of a little stage, five- to seven-month-old babies are shown a little puppet display. First, a bear puppet appears on the stage. Next a screen is lowered concealing the bear from the baby's view. A hand then appears on stage alongside the screen, holding another bear puppet. As the infant watches, the hand containing the second bear goes behind the screen, and reemerges holding nothing (implying that the hand has left the second bear behind). The screen is then removed to reveal either one or two puppets. Amazingly, the baby shows great surprise if, after this addition, only one puppet is revealed. Her surprise comes from the fact that she correctly assumes that when the second puppet was added to the first behind the screen, it should have resulted in two bears. To the baby, seeing only one bear is an unexpected outcome. In other words 1+1 cannot equal 1. Another experiment showed that babies know that 1+1 cannot equal 3. The hand added only one puppet, as before, but when the screen was raised, there were three instead of two bears. Again, babies showed surprise at this impossible outcome, their behaviour indicating that they not only expect to see 'more', but precisely how many more.

A similar experiment demonstrates the infant's ability to subtract. The baby is shown three puppets dancing on the stage, and a screen then appears concealing all the puppets. A hand visibly whisks one of the puppets away from behind the screen, but when the screen is raised, there are still three puppets. Again, the baby shows surprise at this impossible outcome. She counted 3–1, and expected to see two puppets. These experiments demonstrate that by five months, infants are already little mathematicians.

she indicates that she understands that a set of three cars is equal to a set of three flowers. By reacting differently when faced with the smaller set, she shows that she correctly discriminates between the displays based solely on the difference in numbers. But this ability isn't only restricted to what she sees: she also displays early numerical sensitivity to auditory stimuli. Thus, if a baby is played sets of three drumbeats, interspersed with an occasional set of two drumbeats, she will make the same clever distinctions even if both sets are carefully regulated to span the same amount of time.

By five months, the baby is able to use her counting knowledge cross-modally. This means that she can correctly match what she hears to what she sees, and vice versa. So, if she is played a set of two drumbeats and simultaneously presented with visual displays, one containing two items and the other containing three, she will look preferentially at the display containing two. This shows that she can match the quantity of sounds she hears to the quantity of objects she sees. Once again, this numerical discrimination only applies up to and including three. Numbers beyond three exceed the processing capacities of young infants.

A baby's sensitivity to small numbers is quite astounding, but it is a necessary part of her development. It helps her make a very quick assessment of changes in the objects or people around her. So if you change the mobile above her cot from one with three ducks to one with three balls, she will notice the difference of course. But she will equally notice the difference if you change the mobile from three ducks to two ducks. She also uses quantification to track objects. If two little trains go behind the sofa, she will expect to see two trains coming out the other side. If four people come into her bedroom to admire her, and then two leave, she will notice the change in her audience without necessarily having mentally represented precisely what each person looked like.

By five to seven months, the baby's knowledge of small numbers has significantly developed such that she is now able to perform very simple arithmetic. When you think about your tiny, babbling baby, this may seem unbelievable to you. But, amazing as it may appear, her brain is already capable of simple addition and subtraction. She will correctly realise that adding one plus one makes two, or subtracting two from three makes one (*see boxed feature, opposite*).

With the onset of language, by eighteen months the toddler's numerical knowledge becomes more apparent in her everyday behaviour. She is now encouraged to learn to use words like 'one, two, three', and these can act as a useful system with which to represent her expanding knowledge of numbers. Though she may initially use an incorrect sequence of 'number words' when she is counting (for instance she may count four objects as 1…3…4…7), this counting system may actually be governed by a logic based on a series of number-relevant principles. The first principle is one-to-one correspondence: each number word must refer to a different object in the sequence. The next principle is that count words must always be used in the same order. Thus, in the example above, the word 'three' must always refer to the second item in this toddler's counting system. So if she counts the four toys 1…3…4…7 once, she will not then count them as 3…1…4…7 the second time around. Her behaviour isn't that surprising at this stage. There is no logical reason why our language has chosen the particular sound 'two' to represent the concept of 2. This is arbitrary and obviously differs from language to language. A third principle is that of 'item indifference': any item can be called 'three' in her counting system as long as it is the second one counted. The child has got the idea that quantifying involves count words in a fixed sequence. What she still has to learn is to order the count words in the same way that they are ordered

One two, three, four … four holes for four pegs. This little girl is learning about one-to-one correspondence, which forms the basis of her later number knowledge.

in her language (that is, 1, 2, 3, 4 and not 1, 3, 4, 7). The ability to count using the correct sequence of number words is not necessarily indicative of mathematical progress, but rather a sign of growth in language.

The toddler's personal sequence of count words is only temporary, and she will rapidly come to conform to the conventions of her mother tongue. Although some toddlers use the correct sequence from the start, they do not necessarily have a more advanced number system than a child counting in the wrong order, because sometimes the correct sequence is recited more like a poem learned by rote. An eighteen-month-old may even be able correctly to recite all the numbers up to ten, without knowing they have anything to do with counting. Or she may use the labels 'one, two, three, four' for only three objects, counting one of them twice. It is only when the sequence obeys the above three principles that the words play a truly numerical purpose.

If I cruise over there I could stretch up to get the cookie, but if I pull on the ends of the table cloth I can probably reach it as well. And I could always scream and have mum get it for me. There are so many ways to reach my goals. How do I know which solution to choose each time?

By focusing on the goal you're trying to achieve, you'll be able to work out what your options are and decide which action to take. This is a difficult intellectual task. At first you'll try out all the different strategies you can think of until you attain the desired outcome. But with experience, you'll learn how to save time and effort by mentally predicting the outcome of each of your actions without having to try them out first. That way you'll be able to find the best solution for reaching your goal.

PLANNING AHEAD Reasoning, adapting to and controlling the environment is a challenge, even to adults. Yet from very early on, babies show the beginnings of the ability to solve simple problems in order to make the most of their surroundings. Problem solving is by no means straightforward. It involves generating a goal, finding ways of overcoming obstacles to that goal, using the resources available and finally evaluating the outcome of behaviour. It is easy for adults to take this whole process for granted. But when your baby succeeds in pulling a large toy into her playpen, stop and reflect on the complexity of her ingenious behaviour.

During the first six months of life, babies gain a great deal of knowledge not only about the world, but also about their own expanding problem-solving abilities. As early as two months, they are able to work out basic problems such as the need to pull a lever or kick their foot in order to produce music or make a colourful display move. By six months they discover which buttons produce which sounds in an animal toy and are able to operate the right button to get the particular sound they want. As we saw on page 173, by nine months they are able to find a toy hidden under a cover. And by the end of the first year, they can hold a goal in mind and push one object aside to get at another, without getting lost in the subgoal and playing with the first attractive object they encounter. Interestingly, too, problem solving is considerably more successful if the task is embedded in a meaningful context. So, a baby finds a hidden toy more easily in her home environment than in the unfamiliar surroundings of an infant-testing laboratory.

The earliest form of problem solving – used by the infant during the first six months – is 'trial and error'. It is the simplest way of seeking a solution and often emerges merely as part of general exploration. If the baby wants to reach a toy, say, she tries out all the possible strategies available to her to get hold of the toy until by chance one works. At this age she is not able to judge in advance which plans are likely to succeed and which are not. But trial and error does require that the infant keep track of what she has already tried (pulling on a cloth, trying to reach the toy with a stick) in order to progress towards the desired outcome, without going over the same ground again and again. Although trial and error is sometimes the outcome of general play, the two activities are not the same. Scientists found that at both twelve and twenty-four months, children's heart rates decrease during problem solving as compared to play, indicating a significant increase in attention.

A somewhat more advanced form of problem solving involves 'forwards search'. This is sometimes known as 'hill-climbing' and entails using strategies that at each step bring the infant closer to her goal in the most direct way possible. If she wishes to get a bracelet out of a deep hole, she will need to find a sufficiently long stick with a hook on the end. A short stick won't do, nor will a long one without a hook. In order to reason forwards economically, the infant must prioritise the choices of stick available to her and,

Managing your baby's frustration

Infants tend to get terribly despondent when they are unable to achieve their goals. This isn't surprising: imagine how disgruntled you would feel if you could see an enticing toy or snack but, despite repeated efforts, couldn't manage to reach it. If you notice your baby becoming increasingly baffled and annoyed by a problem, encourage her to try again or help her figure out an alternative strategy. Above all, show patience and understanding of her frustration at failure.

As babies get older they tend to show less frustration and instead try out more solutions when encountering barriers to their goals. One study has even noted differences between the sexes: at twelve months, boys tend to cry less

than girls when unable to attain their goals, but by twenty months girls vocalise more for help from others and show less frustration than boys. In general, research has pinpointed the importance of secure bonding (see pages 56–8) in infants' attitudes to problem solving. Those who have established healthy parental attachments are more enthusiastic and less apprehensive about new situations. Mother–child interaction when trying to accomplish a difficult task is also more effective in children who are securely attached. This highlights the importance of infants' emotional stability in the development of their problem-solving skills. So be sure to provide as much general support to your child as you can.

although she cannot yet pinpoint the best option by predicting the outcomes of all possible actions, she is now able to avoid the strategies that she knows in advance won't help her reach her goal. This is a sophisticated mental process and indicates she has achieved a new level of intelligence.

The most complex form of problem solving, called 'means-end analysis', isn't usually seen until after the first birthday. It is the ability to work backwards from the desired outcome to find the most appropriate means or sub-goal to reach a goal. To do this, the toddler has to assess what differentiates the current state from the desired goal state, and the chosen course of action must be aimed at reducing this difference. Although this is a late development, already at ten months babies display the very beginnings of this ability when they tug on a cloth to bring a toy resting on it close enough to reach. One study examined this type of behaviour in babies between nine and eighteen months of age. Infants were shown two cloths, the tips of which were within their reach. An exciting toy was placed on the far end of one of the cloths. Babies of all age groups immediately tried to reach the toy. Those under nine months pulled indiscriminately on both cloths. But most infants between ten and twelve months only grabbed the cloth on which the toy was placed and pulled it towards themselves. They also knew not to pull on the cloth if the toy was beside rather than on it. Problem solving in under eighteen-month-olds is nonetheless limited. When three cloths were presented, only eighteen-month-olds consistently pulled the right cloth. In other words, somewhere towards the latter part of their second year, toddlers can assess increasingly complex problem-solving situations and plan the appropriate action or actions required to solve them without engaging in tedious trial and error.

Toddlers also have the capacity to understand the goals of others. In one study, for example, eighteen-month-olds were shown on video an adult who tried but failed to perform a number of target actions such as putting a lid on a tin. They were never shown the successful acts, only seeing the adult fail to get the lid on. Yet the toddlers imitated the successful act rather than the failed attempt, indicating that they interpreted the adult's action as goal-oriented rather than observing simply what was demonstrated.

At ten months, this little girl knows that the easiest way to reach her favourite toy is by tugging the blanket on which it sits.

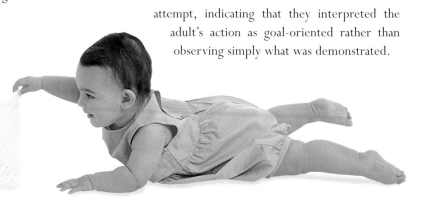

LOOKING AHEAD **As toddlers' intelligence develops, their imagination, fantasy and curiosity play an increasingly important role in their lives. New forms of play emerge which stretch the boundaries of the here and now, and even of reality. They also no longer accept the world as it is, but want to understand why things function the way they do.**

DEVELOPING IMAGINATION The onset of pretend play is a developmental milestone. Usually this occurs around eighteen months. Babies no longer see an object simply in terms of its functional use (a comb is for brushing hair), but begin to appreciate the potential symbolic meaning that an object can take (a comb can be anything you pretend it is). This allows them to *invent* rather than just imitate during play. Why is this such an important step? Well, let's take the example of using a banana as a pretend telephone. To play this game, the toddler has to set aside everything she knows about bananas – that they are yellow and soft inside, that they can be peeled and eaten, unlike the phone. For the moment, she must temporarily replace this reality about bananas with the things she knows about telephones – that they are rigid, have buttons and usually a wire, make noises and let you speak to people who aren't there. This involves tricky mental gymnastics! By placing reality on hold, the child achieves what is called 'meta-representation' of the world. In other words, she manages to lift the internal image of the world she has formed in her mind to a higher level where it doesn't simply represent reality, but also an imagined world. And she must do this without at the same time losing what she knows to be really true about phones and bananas.

Through this complicated process children are able to hold and utilise two representations of the world simultaneously – one of the real world, and one of an imagined world – without mixing the two. Pretend play can become very elaborate in time, with complex events and situations acted out, and the adoption of different roles (doctors and nurses, or cowboys and indians). Children use symbolic play not only to broaden their exploration of the world, but also to work out the rules of social interaction. Through play, they try out role-reversal. For instance, what happens if baby tells off mummy? Or if dad asks baby for permission to eat chocolate cake? Such games give the child a stage upon which she can act out emotionally difficult situations as well.

Lately, I've found it fun to play strange games like brushing my doll's hair with a pencil. I even played at phoning dad using a banana. Am I losing my sense of reality?

No, of course you're not. When you're playing these games, you know that a banana isn't a telephone and that the pencil is not a brush. You're just using your imagination to make your games even more fun. This is actually a big step in your development: you are starting to explore the idea of symbols by making an arbitrary object represent something else. The way you play goes through many different stages, indicating that you're gaining many important new social skills.

Fantasy play also involves a fabricated reality but includes unreal things such as giants, aliens or fairies. In this case, the child does not symbolise but rather invents. This is just as important a skill, as it shows the ability to use imagination not only to alter but also to create. It is therefore important to give room to your child's fantasies and not treat them as untruths.

Why shouldn't I touch the fire?... Why does the lady say no?... Why can't I have any more sweets?... Why do mum and dad get irritated when I ask them so many questions?

Because...because...because their answers never seem to satisfy you! During this period you want to understand everything about objects, events and people. And you've just discovered a nice, short word: 'why'. Initially, your parents will be delighted with your inquisitiveness and answer you patiently. But when one question turns into a long string of 'whys?', they soon lose their enthusiasm. Try taking a little time to digest one answer before going on to your next query.

THE THIRST FOR KNOWLEDGE Some time between 24 and 36 months, children start to ask questions about the way the social and physical worlds function. These questions appear later than 'where' questions (about the location of things) and 'what' questions (about the names of things). This is because asking *why* something happens requires more complex cognitive processing. The 'why?' period can be quite a harassing time for parents because your child never seems pacified by the responses you provide and continues to ask yet another 'why?' It is as if at times children think there must be a reason for everything, but don't know where to stop in the chain. Furthermore, they may not always understand your explanation, and go on to the next 'why?' to prevent the dialogue ending. Patience is very important, for your child's intellectual curiosity is now at its zenith, and your encouragement to explore these questions will have a positive effect on her subsequent development.

Early questions are usually people-oriented and about the social rules that restrict their behaviour. Your child may challenge why certain actions, such as asking someone why they are fat, are prohibited, or question the causes of emotional states, for example why someone is sad. Later, this extends to questions about the functioning of objects and how cause and effect are related. They may ask why cats mew and dogs bark, or why telephones ring. If parents respond to their child's question by asking her what *she* thinks, the child may initially focus on human-like motivations rather than physical cause-and-effect. So, if the child is asked why ice cream melts, she might reply 'because it wants to'. However, children rapidly move beyond this and try to provide an explanation for everything in terms of the laws of the world.

At times children's questions can be not only frustrating but really difficult to answer at an understandable level. Here's a typical exchange: Child: 'Why can't I walk on the hot sand?' Mum: 'Because it will burn your feet.' 'Why will it burn my feet?' 'Because it is hot and your feet are delicate.' 'Why is it hot?' 'Because the sun has been warming it all morning.' 'Why are my feet

'Daddy, Daddy, why is your shadow on that side and where's my shadow gone?' The inquisitive toddler uses endless questions to develop an understanding of the world.

delicate?' 'Because your skin is soft.' 'Why is my skin soft?' 'BECAUSE IT IS!' One sometimes wonders if these exchanges are more about keeping a conversation going than really finding out why things are the way they are.

Surprisingly, even when your child may not at first understand your answers, she still stores away a lot of the information gathered in these interminable question-and-answer sessions, and may return to the topic later to clarify the explanations given. The 'why?' questions are a sign that your toddler has progressed beyond simply observing the world and accepting what she sees as fact to seeking the reasons behind what she observes. In doing so, she is distinguishing her intellectual capacity from that of all other species. In other words, she is moving beyond observation to generating hypotheses about why things happen the way that they do, and realising that adults are sources of rich information about life. From then on, the world is her oyster. As she continues to develop intellectually, she will discover school, the joy of books and dictionaries, the Internet, and a host of other ways of answering her questions about the world. She is on the road to becoming a mature thinker.

Index

ACKNOWLEDGEMENTS

Picture credits

Page 1 Tony Stone Images; **7** Tony Stone Images; **8** Tony Stone Images; **10** Petit Format/Prof. E. Symonds/SPL; **11** Image Bank/Carol Kohen; **12** The Stock Market; **15** Derek Bromhall/Oxford Scientific Films; **16** Tony Stone Images; **19** Collections/Anthea Sieveking; **21 above** Image Bank/Steve Allen; **21 below** Collections/Anthea Sieveking; **22** Petit Format/Nestle/SPL; **23** The Stock Market; **25** Tony Stone Images; **26** Image Bank/Ken Huang; **27** Acuson images courtesy of Prof. M. Hansmann, Bonn, Germany; **28** Tony Stone Images; **30** Tony Stone Images; **31** Collections/Sandra Lousada; **32** Mehau Kulyk/SPL; **34** Collections/Anthea Sieveking; **35** Taeka Henstra/Petit Format/SPL; **37** Keith/Custom Medical Stock Photo/SPL; **38** Telegraph Colour Library; **43** Tony Stone Images; **44** Tony Stone Images; **46** Collections/Sandra Lousada; **47** Tony Stone Images; **51** Mother & Baby Picture Library/emap élan; **55** Tony Stone Images; **56** Tony Stone Images; **59** Tony Stone Images; **60** Telegraph Colour Library; **61** Tony Stone Images; **64** Tony Stone Images; **69** Tony Stone Images; **70** Angela Hampton/Family Life Pictures; **71** Collections/Anthea Sieveking; **72** Collections/Fiona Pragoff; **76** Ace Photo Agency; **78** Angela Hampton/Family Life Pictures; **79** Collections/Sandra Lousada; **87** Tony Stone Images; **88** Tony Stone Images; **89** Collections/Fiona Pragoff; **90** Angela Hampton/Family Life Pictures; **91** Tony Stone Images; **93** The Stock Market; **96** Tony Stone Images; **103** Collections/Anthea Sieveking; **106** Tony Stone Images; **107** Bubbles/Ian West; **108** Images Colour Library; **110** Collections/Sandra Lousada; **111** Images Colour Library; **112** Tony Stone Images; **119** Collections/Anthea Sieveking; **121** Collections/Sandra Lousada; **123** Tony Stone Images; **125** Tony Stone Images; **128** Collections/Fiona Pragoff; **129** Collections/Sandra Lousada; **130 above** Angela Hampton/Family Life Pictures; **130 below** Ron Sutherland/SPL; **132** Images Colour Library; **134** Mother & Baby Picture Library/EmapElan; **135** Tony Stone Images; **141** Telegraph Colour Library; **145 left** Collections/Fiona Pragoff; **148** Tony Stone Images; **149** Collections/Sandra Lousada; **152** Ace Photo Agency; **154** Images Colour Library; **155** Collections/Sandra Lousada; **161** Angela Hampton/Family Life Pictures; **162** Collections/Anthea Sieveking; **166** Explorer/Robert Harding Picture Library; **168** Angela Hampton/Family Life Pictures; **169** Collections/Sandra Lousada; **176** Collections/Sandra Lousada; **178** Angela Hampton/Family Life Pictures; **183** Collections/ Anthea Sieveking; **189** Angela Hampton/Family Life Pictures.

Author acknowledgements

We would like to thank Amy Carroll who first approached us with the idea for this book, and Rachel Aris who kept us on our toes in her role as editor. Our appreciation also goes to our respective partners, Gideon and Marek, for their unbelievable patience during this very busy writing period.

Carroll & Brown acknowledgements

We would very much like to thank: Kym Menzies and Rachael Atfield for hair and make-up; Lee McPherson and Alex Franklin for photographic assistance; Sandra Schneider for picture research; and Madeline Weston for the index. Special thanks also to Stephanie Strickland for the illustrations.